Metaphor: Its Therapeutic Use and Construction

Metaphor: Its Therapeutic Use and Construction

A Professional Guide to Using Metaphor in
Psychotherapy and Counseling

Martin Cohen

Foreword by David H. Rosen

RESOURCE *Publications* · Eugene, Oregon

METAPHOR: ITS THERAPEUTIC USE AND CONSTRUCTION
A Professional Guide to Using Metaphor in Psychotherapy and Counseling

Resource Publications
An Imprint of Wipf and Stock Publishers
199 W. 8th Ave., Suite 3
Eugene, OR 97401

www.wipfandstock.com

PAPERBACK ISBN: 978-1-5326-4471-9
HARDCOVER ISBN: 978-1-5326-4472-6
EBOOK ISBN: 978-1-5326-4473-3

Manufactured in the U.S.A.

To Gabriela
Who found me when I most needed to be found and devoted
her love and encouragement to start me on a path toward
wholeness. Writing this book has helped move me along.

Contents

Foreword

I AM A CLINICIAN who likes metaphor. I use them in therapy. So, this book is welcomed. Recently, I saw a new patient, and I thought that she was the sun sparkling. Obviously, it was too soon to share this metaphor with her. As this book clearly outlines, you first have to develop a meaningful relationship with the patient before disclosing such an analogy.

This manuscript would have aided and will aid me in developing and utilizing metaphor with patients. With this book, one cannot only understand metaphor, one can also learn how to construct them for healing relationships. This is a text that will assist clinicians of all disciplines. It is a great honor to endorse this volume, as it will help many on their healing journeys.

In my work as a Jungian psychoanalyst, I often use many of the metaphors discussed in this book. I tell stories, anecdotes, fairy-tales, fables, and parables that relate to the person's problem. For example, I have used the Hansel and Gretel fairy-tale when a patient was suffering from a severe negative mother complex. This tale helps the person analyze their conflict with a devouring-mother. As a child, a mother was smothered with the adoration of their maternal grandmother. She recalled her mother saying, "You're so good, I could just gobble you up."

This book is a natural one for me to endorse and recommend. I applaud Dr. Cohen for writing his treatise, which ought to assist many.

David H. Rosen, MD
Eugene, Oregon

Preface

LET'S BEGIN WITH THE important question: Why do you need this book? My best answer is to affirm the large number of treatment techniques most mental health professionals use successfully from their tool kit. At the same time, I know that most clinicians* fail to take full advantage of a most valuable tool: the extended psychotherapeutic metaphor. My research attempts to gather information on the current status of therapeutic metaphor usage confirms the lack of use of this tool. I strongly maintain that an increased knowledge of the process of therapeutic metaphor utilization and construction can increase your effectiveness as a clinician.

This book investigates the contemporary research on the extended metaphor to determine how it can be used most effectively in a therapeutic setting. It seeks to do so by presenting the underpinnings of understanding and using therapeutic metaphor. Perhaps most importantly, this book provides you with a model for constructing original metaphors that includes the therapeutic components necessary to effect meaningful change in your clients. This is especially important when we consider that each client is an individual and requires treatment specific to his or her needs.

The therapeutic metaphor is an intervention by the clinician that is presented to the client in story form: as anecdotes, parables, fairytales, etc. Its non-threatening presentation can create new insights and different, or original, perspectives on a client's approach to problem resolution. There is abundant research on *literary* metaphor: One might open up a Holy Bible or turn to Aristotle or Coleridge to experience the metaphorical harmony of the universe

---

* I will be using the designation "clinician," a qualified person involved in the treatment of clients, for "therapist/psychotherapist" and "counselor" throughout this book.

touching upon the mind and heart. We clinicians are less fortunate. Relevant work on the extended psychotherapeutic metaphor is sparse. In "Metaphor: A review of the Psychological Literature," Richard M. Billow (1975) concludes, "Given the scarcity of systematic investigation of metaphor it is not surprising that theory is incomplete and research is non-conclusive." Paivio and Walsh (See Ortony 1975, 307) concur: "Much of the psychological research on metaphor was not directed at a really fundamental problems in the area." Moser (1998, 21), in turn, points out, "The analysis of metaphors is a classical research theme in linguistics, but has received very little attention in psychological research so far. . . . A further and new definition of metaphor models has to be developed in order to achieve a reliable operationalization of metaphor models. Here, further systematization and methodological development is still needed."

The contributions of Milton H. Erickson and David Gordon stand as valuable contributions to the construction and use of therapeutic metaphors. Unfortunately, their system is narrow and restrictive because it is presented within the boundaries of hypnotherapy and Neurolinguistic Programming. Thus it is less applicable to other psychotherapy treatment styles. I propose a model of therapeutic metaphor comprehension and construction that can accommodate mental health professionals working in the major systems such as psychodynamic, cognitive, behavioral, gestalt, marriage and family therapy, co-counseling, etc. and using metaphors in their regular clinical practice. To remedy the lack of "systematic investigation" of the use of metaphor in clinical practice, this book provides the immediate concrete information that can help you to employ this important tool effectively.

This book will provide you with a basic understanding of how metaphor can enhance your regime of therapeutic techniques. You will learn:

- The usefulness of therapeutic metaphors for the client, for the clinician

- The elements in metaphors that make them therapeutic

- The utility (or usefulness) of therapeutic metaphors for the client, for the clinician
- When, and for which client, a metaphor is most effective
- What issues are most conducive to metaphoric presentation
- Which of a client's personality factors affect the way you construct a metaphor
- What type of person responds best to metaphor

A detailed description of the components used to create original therapeutic metaphors will instruct you in a step-by-step fashion. You will find two full-length annotated metaphors along with many metaphor examples that help illustrate the text. This book aims to help readers in all treatment modalities effectively use the extended metaphor as a therapeutic tool, and involves explaining the theoretical basis for its use and how to construct original metaphors applicable to your individual clients.

Acknowledgements

It is an honor *to have* David Rosen, MD *write the foreword to this book. I am grateful for his generous time and clear and kind words.*

I also wish to express my appreciation to clinicians, Charles Kuell, Karen Michael Peoples, Peter N. Alevizos, and Joan Hersh *for contributing metaphors to help make this book possible.*

My thanks to Linda C. Saisselin, Teresa Montes, Hope Lane, Judith Castro, Zanne Miller, and Tatiana Sporea, *who have given me a more objective view of how other therapists can use and benefit from this book.*

I owe special thanks to my copy editor, Jane Ganter, *for her tireless work to pull this book together.*

Introduction

A FORMER CLIENT SURPRISED me one evening with an excited, albeit slightly confused, telephone call. I had been seeing him in therapy for several months and there didn't seem to be much progress in our sessions. I had experienced Richard as extremely defensive and unwilling to deal with any of the issues he had come to therapy to resolve. He had been resisting direct confrontation with his underlying problems so I decided to take a different approach; one I believe resulted in that propitious telephone call.

Richard was speaking rapidly—he hardly spoke at all during our sessions. He said that he had been sitting at dinner and, for "no apparent reason," remembered a story I told him a day earlier. What he had paid very little (conscious) attention to initially now had a special meaning. It seemed to make the right connection for him to move him to action. Richard said that he felt like he was in a trance (trance-acted?) and proceeded to "take care of the business with my girlfriend just like the guy in the story solved his problem." He went on to say, "I guess I needed to look at this thing a little differently . . . in a new way. It makes a lot of sense to me now!"

I knew immediately what prompted Richard's change of attitude and opened a new door to his problem. I had used an indirect method to communicate a concept that I wanted him to consider. I did that by relating a story, a metaphor that was sufficiently non-threatening for him to store away in his unconscious. I had presented a metaphor that I felt would benefit my client if he would consider how it might apply to his situation. The intellectual aspect of the concept seemed to have little immediate impact in the session. That is not unusual. (Richard chose not to even discuss it!) However, I began to notice nonverbal signs of interest as I proceeded with the metaphor. His body language indicated that he was indeed listening carefully to what I was saying, but his voice expressed the not uncommon response, "What does this have to do with anything?"

Indeed, what does telling stories, anecdotes, fairy tales, fables, or parables have to do with the psychotherapeutic process? I found that I was using more and more metaphors in my work without really considering the process. My clients were experiencing more successful outcomes when I added the metaphor to my various therapeutic techniques. I knew that something positive was happening, so I continued using metaphors whenever they seemed appropriate. Then I discovered the work of Haley, Gordon, and Lankton's use of the metaphor as a teaching device and a therapeutic tool (Haley, 2014; Gordon, 1975; Lankton, 1980). I was fascinated to realize that I was using so powerful a therapeutic technique that my clients improved even with my limited knowledge of the process. I felt compelled to learn as much as I could about how to use metaphors more effectively. I developed my own model of constructing and using the therapeutic metaphor, a process I now want to share with you.

My preliminary research for this book involved speaking to many clinicians who said that they use metaphors as a therapeutic technique. I realized that, with a few exceptions, those I interviewed had, at best, a limited understanding of how to use the metaphor in a treatment plan. That was no surprise; it correlated with my own limited knowledge in the area. Interestingly, our lack of understanding didn't prevent any of us from using anecdotes or stories whenever we thought that they would fit a client's situation.

Many of the reasons the clinicians gave for using metaphors underlined the need for greater understanding of the therapeutic process involved. Some typical responses were:

"It's just something I use as well as any other technique of therapy. I don't do anything special."

"Metaphors usually make what we're talking about more clear."

"I usually use an example when I think that the client is not getting the point. It may be a story or similar situation another client experienced."

"I have always told anecdotes to clients. I don't usually think about it . . . I just do it!"

I believe that few clinicians make optimal use of the tool that could have a powerful impact on the therapeutic process. With a better understanding of the pragmatic underpinnings of the therapeutic metaphor, and have the ability to construct original metaphors for your clients, you will be even more effective in your practice.

1   Understanding Metaphor

Metaphor is both important and odd—its importance odd and its
oddity important.
—Nelson Goodman, *Language of Art*

As philosophy grows more abstract we think increasingly by means
of metaphors that we profess not to be relying on.
—I. A. Richards, *Life and Work*

Each story conveys a different view of reality and represents a special
way of seeing.
—Donald A. Schon, "Generative Metaphor"

A BASIC AIM OF the physical and social sciences is to find general explanations of natural events; usually such explanations are
called theories. The field of metaphor is no different in its efforts
to search out not just the meaning of metaphor, but also a theory
that will help to explain this multi–faceted phenomena. Over time,
academicians have developed, criticized, and expanded theories of
metaphor, what Kövecses (2002, p. xiii) calls the "cognitive linguistic study of metaphor". They regard metaphor as an important part
of life, discourse and learning, and developed theories to more
completely explain this phenomenon (see especially Kovecses
(2nd ed.), Reynolds and Schwartz 1983, Lakeoff and Johnson
1978, Black 1962, Tourangeau and Sternberg 1982, Torneke 2017).

Innumerable explanations of metaphor come from Aristotle
—"Metaphor, is by far the most important thing to master"—to

Frost, "All thinking is metaphorical." I have been selective and diligently tried to choose the works that best illuminate the subject. Let's begin with a useful review of the understanding of metaphor. According to Tourangeau and Sternberg (1982), the metaphor is a comparison in which one term (the tenor or subject of the comparison) is asserted to bare a partial resemblance (the ground of the comparison) to something else (the vehicle), to sustain a literal comparison. Put more simply, their comparison theory asserts that metaphorical utterances involve a comparison or similarity between two or more objects. For example, the metaphor, "David is a lion in battle," compares two figures of unlike nature. Yet in some respect they share similar characteristics. Both are courageous; both fight ferociously and are unconquerable in battle. This thing to which the first object is compared is to be understood in some "transferred" sense. In that sense, David is a lion.

Many authorities advance the notion that the use of metaphor can generate new insights and provide new perspectives. The following examples may suffice to support this contention. Ortony (1975, p. 45) argues for their long tradition as teaching/learning devices:

> Metaphors, and their close relatives, similes and analogies, have been used as teaching devices since the earliest writings of civilized man. The dialogues of Plato are full of them; . . . there is the cave metaphor to *The Republic* designed to illuminate various levels of knowledge, The Bible is another good source of metaphor, arid, of course, metaphor is the stock-in-trade of poets and writers. The widespread use of metaphor in even the earliest 'teaching texts' however, suggests that . . . metaphor is an essential ingredient of communication and consequently of great educational value.

N. L. Smith (1981, p. 25) concludes that "the utility of metaphors can be viewed as fully established as a heuristic device: a teaching/learning method which encourages a person to discover for him or herself solutions to their life experiences. What has not been established or developed is a comprehensible and employable methodology for utilizing and constructing therapeutic metaphors."

Burke (1945, pp. 503-504) emphasizes the metaphor as an especially good technique for providing perspective.

> Metaphor is a device for seeing something in terms of something else. It brings out the *thisness* of that, or the *thatness* of this. If we employ the word 'character' as a general term for whatever can be thought of as distinct (any thing, pattern, situation, structure, nature, person, object, act, role, process, event, etc.), then we can say that metaphor tells us something about one character as considered from the point of view of another character. And to consider A from the point of view of B is, of course, to use B as a perspective upon A.

Wallace (1982, p. 32) describes the magical quality of metaphor: "Metaphors work in bewildering ways and do a variety of jobs, sometimes so completely that no conscious analysis can follow them. They may illustrate, explain, emphasize, heighten, communicate information or ideas, or carry a tome, feeling or attitude."

Kopp (1971, p. 7) addresses the old philosophical question, "How do we know?" He answers the "how" by "knowing (the world) metaphorically." He explains that we "depend on an intuitive grasp of situations, in which we are open to the symbolic dimensions of experience, opened to the multiple meanings that may all coexist, giving extra shades of meaning to each other."

To give us a more lyrical look at metaphor, writing on the metaphors and parables of gurus, Kopp (1972, pp. 1718) defines metaphor as

> a way of speaking in which one thing is expressed in terms of another, whereby this bringing together throws a new light on the character of what is being described . . . for our purposes we will take metaphor in the broad sense, as denoting any kind of comparison as a basis for the kind of illumination we call poetic.

The above examples are aimed to orient and acquaint you with the most acceptable—and, perhaps, most popular—theories of metaphor. It appears from a review of the literature that the foundation of metaphoric understanding is grounded in, or at least touches deeply upon, social, philosophical, and linguistic patterns of society, as well as the psychological domain. This being the case, familiarity with these foundations can be helpful to you as a clinician to fully incorporate a working understanding of metaphorical intervention into your therapy process.

2 Therapeutic Metaphor
A Special Use of Language

Language is vitally metaphorical.
—Shelley, "A Defense of Poetry"

The most fruitful and modern criticism is a rediscovery and recovery
of the importance of metaphor.
—Clench Brooks, *Irony as a Principle of Structure*

All our truth, or all but a few fragments,
is won by metaphor.
—C. S. Lewis, *Selected Literary Essays*

METAPHOR, AS A THERAPEUTIC tool, is a concept borrowed from
many ancient and modern disciplines whose practitioners have
pondered its meaning, use, and contribution for centuries. While
philosophers have been speculating about the nature of metaphor
since at least the time of Aristotle, the psychotherapeutic community only recently began to seriously reinvestigate the subject matter. An increasing amount of research and investigation has been
conducted since the late 1980s in an attempt to define metaphor,
determine its function, locate its academic domain and articulate
its construction.

Although it happens that any meaning can be expressed
precisely and accurately in a direct way, as a function of the com-
municator's abilities, I believe that once the same message is com-
municated metaphorically, we are dealing in another dimension.

To illustrate this point, I propose two descriptions of a person accepting a bribe. The first is a fairly clear and articulate expression of a direct communication. The second produces equality that brings the listener into that new dimension.

> Even as I was accepting the money, I knew I was in for grave consequences. I really understood at the deepest level what a terrible mistake I was making and yet I took the money anyway.

> I could feel the barbed hook slipping down into my mouth. Suddenly, and before I could do a thing about it, I felt a violent jolt that set the hook deep into my jaw. I was hooked and wriggling helplessly from another man's pole.

Something happens to transform the meaning and it becomes understood, sometimes dramatically, differently. Differently, in that a feeling, emotion, and an affective state are produced that influences one's outlook or relatedness to the issue being considered. The metaphor engenders this affective state that joins with the cognitive component. The client thus obtains an alternate frame of reference that is provided by the metaphorical form and structure. It may be important here to briefly compare some of the major manifestations of direct interpretations and metaphorical devices in terms of similarities and differences.

Direct Interpretation and Therapeutic Metaphor

	Direct Interpretation	Therapeutic Metaphor
1	A direct interpretation creates resistance putting up defense mechanisms to protect against a fragile self.	A direct interpretation can be ignored by the unconscious, thus heading off any need to protect against impending anxiety. It also prevents the "planting of a seed" in the cultivation of an unacceptable concept becoming integrated into the client's belief system.

Direct Interpretation	Therapeutic Metaphor
2 The language of an interpretation should reflect the directness and accuracy of the intended meaning.	It is precisely because metaphor describes one situation as a function of a seemingly very different situation, that the client is permitted to find his own way interpreting the language, reflecting on couched references, and opens new possibilities of dealing with the situation to gain the intended meaning.
3 Interpretations are to be delivered in such a manner that gives the client the opportunity to accept or rejected which may cause conflict between clinician and client and may even lead to placating the clinician.	Since the intended meaning is being expressed in terms of something else, there is ample opportunity for the unconscious to reject the intended meaning without it being an issue. There is no reason to either placate or offend the clinician for a meaning that was not directly delivered.
4 Too many points covered in an interpretation serve only to scatter and confuse. The client can usually consider and integrate small portions at any one time, especially if they are anxiety producing and are unacceptable to the self.	This is not a problem with the metaphor because it relies upon the unconscious to pick and choose those points it will consider and integrate into the self. If too much anxiety is attached to a particular piece, it will remain "unattended to" until the client is ready to consider acceptance.
5 Accusations or moral judgments are to be avoided. Any interpretations that may bring defensiveness, embarrassment, or a sense of ridicule can only result in greater resistance.	Metaphors are virtually value free and will not evoke feelings of defensiveness, or ridicule as a function of the metaphor itself. All feelings evoked from the client experiencing a metaphor will be a function of the allowable insight that is derived solely from the metaphor.

Clinicians have discovered that metaphor occurs not only in creative acts involving aesthetic imagination, but also plays a vital role in facilitating the effectiveness of psychotherapy and more general problem-solving. If you are going to begin to more consciously utilize this technique, it is wise and useful to acquaint yourself with some of the theories, uses, and functions of the psychotherapeutic metaphor. Most recently discussions on the metaphor, its use and relevance, have also appeared in the psycho-therapeutic literature. It is also important to understand that many of the questions, themes, consensus, and arguments on metaphor in the psychotherapeutic field have been investigated in various other disciplines. It's interesting to observe that most studies and debates on the subject fall into the same categories as those in the literature in many multidisciplinary fields. This repetition suggests that until fundamental questions are answered about the meta-phor, basic patterns of inquiry will repeat themselves. It is, there-fore, my goal to shed enough light on these fundamental questions concerning the extended therapeutic metaphor to give you the ability to successfully use and construct this important tool.

Although discussion in the field of psychology has at times been esoteric and problematic, the understanding of extended therapeutic metaphor can be reduced to three simple areas: what it is, how it works, and its psychological status.

(a) We can recognize an extended therapeutic metaphor by its imaginative nature and story form. Once we have identified it, our appreciation of its nonliteral speech differs from the way we hear literal speech. (b) How it works involves questions of creativ-ity and language, the mechanisms of metaphor, and the nature of its meaning. (c) Its psychological status is simply its role in our clinical disciplines.

Bunny Duhl (1983, p. 128) and others at the Boston Family Institute state that metaphor is the "transposing of an image or as-sociation from one state or arena of meaning to another, highlight-ing similarities, differences and/or ambiguities. . . . The metaphor is the linkage of meaning—that which connects any two events, ideas, characteristics, modes."

With the use of metaphor, Lankton and Lankton (1983, p. 160) confide that "the therapy session proceeds and the client op-erates from his or her personal meaning while attending less and less on instructions and direction from the clinician. In this regard, indirect suggestion seems to be far less manipulative than a direct approach, since it offers a wide range of options to the client."

Kaplan (1964, p. 228) links the metaphor specifically to the scientific development of psychoanalytic theory:

> There is the familiar hydrodynamic metaphor in psycho-analysis, with the id as a reservoir having several 'outlets' which can lower internal pressure, which in turn are countered by forces of repression, and so on. Freud also uses a societal analogy, with a 'censor,' an authoritarian 'superego,' internal 'conflicts' and the like.

Paivio and Walsh (1979, p. 309) describe what motivates the use of metaphor to convey information to the hearer:

> A metaphor provides a compact way of representing the subject of cognitive and perceptual features that are salient to it. A metaphor allows large 'chunks' of infor-mation to be converted or transferred from the vehicle to the topic. . . . Through imagery, metaphors provide vivid and, therefore, memorable and emotion-arousing representation of perceived experience.

David Gordon (1978, p. 18), one of the more sophisticated theorists on the subject of metaphors, provides a succinct defini-tion: "Metaphor is a form of fairytales, and anecdotes used by the clinician to assist in change. Metaphors are a form of indirect ex-pression capable of assessing in its listener intended content with-out the content being explicitly identified. Thereby the listener is offered a new and more useful perspective."

Gordon also extended the meaning of metaphor beyond telling stories and anecdotes. He created for his clients real-world experiences that were actually metaphors: asking a couple to climb Squaw Peak to gain a new perspective-

I would like to emphasize how extended metaphors func-tion as a therapeutic tool by summarizing some of Lenrow's ideas (1966, pp. 146–148).

- Metaphor models for a client the clinician's willingness to try out novel ways of looking at behavior.

- Metaphors function to simplify events in terms of scheme, or a concept, that emphasizes some properties more than others. They serve to shake-up old habits of thinking;

- The concrete referents of metaphorical language give communications an intimate or personal quality. Metaphors usually refer to (a) sensory experience (sounds, taste), (b) visual impressions of concrete objects, (c) specific roles (organ grinders, stepchild, priest), or (d) specific accouterments of a role (security blanket, brass knocker).

- Metaphors have a half playful, half serious quality. Clinicians can talk about intimate things without being intrusive or evoking avoidance.

Most of the initial work on the therapeutic metaphor seems to come from followers of Milton H. Erickson, one of the foremost authorities on hypnotherapy and brief psychotherapy. Zeig (1980, pp. 7–14) describes some of the values of using metaphors to achieve the goals of therapy. He categorizes them as: (a) to lessen resistance to change—a decidedly non-threatening approach; (b) to make or illustrate a point by "tagging" the memory—they make the idea more memorable; (c) to suggest solutions by telling a "parallel" or multiple "metaphor"; (d) to get people to see themselves in a realistic way; (e) to seed ideas and increase motivation by increasing positive expectancy; (f) to therapeutically control the relationship; (g) to embed—a form of indirect suggestion; (h) to reframe and redefine a problem. Zeig (1980) describes some additional uses—such as an ego-building technique, to remind a person of her/his own resources, and to desensitize a fear—and describes how Erickson uses the metaphor diagnostically and to establish rapport. It is evident that the usefulness of any therapy technique is a function of the ability and creativity of the individual clinician. It is also evident that metaphor has a variety of uses in the therapeutic process, and that you can improve your skills by employing them.

Metaphors can also function well in small therapeutic groups. Although stories often appear unrelated to the group at first, they help conceptualize the problems facing group members and offer structures for member interaction. Members become more aware of the assumptions guiding their behavior. Collective dramatic talk allows members to access the collective thoughts that bind members together and limits and directs their behavior.

Therapy is a developmental process and is conducted in phases. Metaphor can be used in any phase of the treatment process and in any modality of psychotherapy. There are no known contraindications for their use. Certain operations are common to all modes of psychotherapy, notably diagnosis, establishing empathetic rapport, and carrying out a treatment plan where the use of metaphor can be most effective. Lankton (1980, p. 153) supports this use of extended metaphor in diverse modalities, stating "the diversity of therapeutic models and the fact that each of them in its own way helps bring about change in clients, points out the power of metaphor to shape individual experience."

To sum up, more generally the extended therapeutic metaphor can be understood as a teaching/learning story that a client can find meaning in as it relates to his or her life. By decreasing resistance, metaphor helps clients better recognize parts of themselves that may be too uncomfortable—even painful—to accept from a direct intervention. In addition to being non-threatening to the client, metaphor can be most engaging, capturing the attention of the client in an informal and genial manner. Lankton (1980, p. 161) adds, "Knowing that a treatment metaphor is just that—a story designed to help expand the client's own story—sets us free to use any metaphor that is appropriate and to even make up stories that are specifically suited to the client's needs." Most importantly, its contents or message/learning is presented, by definition, in a non-threatening manner that creates new insights and different, or original, perspectives in terms of problem resolution by the client. You, then, function as a storyteller (or "teacher" in some parlance) who has at your disposal an important tool to motivate and assist the client to manifest constructive change.

As professional communicators, we listen closely to what our clients are saying on both a metaphorical and a literal level.

People intuitively communicate metaphorically. If this is the case for the client, it must be equally true for the clinician. With this basic understanding we are free to develop a system for reaching this important center for cognitive, behavioral, and emotional change in our clients. We can explicitly address the metaphorical thought process to affect ideas and help initiate change in our clients. When you incorporate this comprehensive and practical method to utilize and construct therapeutic metaphors, you will have an invaluable tool that can dramatically improve the positive outcomes for your clients.

3   Milton H. Erickson, et al.

For the student of languages and thought, metaphor is an eclipse.
Metaphor obscures its literal and commonplace aspects while per-
mitting a new and subtle understanding to emerge.
—Paivio and Walsh, *Psychological Processes in Metaphor*

And what therefore is truth? A mobile army of metaphors. To know
is merely to work with one's favorite metaphors.
—Nietzsche, *Philosophical Writings*

Metaphors provide the glue that holds a framework together with the
living experiences.
—Lankton and Lankton, *The Answer Within*

NO DISCUSSION ABOUT THE therapeutic metaphor would be complete without a shout out to Milton H. Erickson. One needs to
begin with the work of Erickson—as seen through such followers
as Jay Haley, Jeffrey Zeig, and David Gordon—to comment on the
existing models available to clinicians and why they are insufficient
for most mental health practitioners. The use of metaphor, which
usually took the form of an anecdote called a "teaching story," is a
technique Erickson commonly employed to facilitate change within his method of hypnotherapy. However, it cannot be generally
held as a model for most of us to practice the Ericksonian brand
of psychotherapy. Unlike Freud or Jung, among others, Erickson
has no theory of personality that requires a specific approach to

change and growth. Erickson's therapy method is indirection. As Zeig (1980, p. xx) points out, "He was a firm believer that an explicit theory of personality would limit the psychotherapist and make the psychotherapist more rigid." Erickson does Erickson, and there can be no duplicators to get the same results. His use of extended metaphors (anecdotes) is a spontaneous and natural part of Milton H. Erickson and his approach to his clients. His "nonverbal behavior, his intonations, his laugh and sense of aliveness unfortunately cannot be reproduced" (Zeig, xxviii). This is the way he communicates his cure. The "cure," however, seems to be inside Erickson rather than inside the client, and Erickson finds effective ways (hypnotherapy) to inculcate it into the client. It is not my intention to pass judgment on Erickson's techniques (in many quarters Erickson's influence is thought to equal Freud's), but to explain why I was never able to learn enough about metaphors from him or his followers. Ericksonian hypnotherapy has certainly been shown effective for Erickson, but there was, unfortunately, only one Milton H. Erickson!*

As a therapist, I don't resonate with Nuerolinguestic Programming. I have never connected with the NLP ideas of Bandler and Grender (1975), nor have I connected with the scholarly work of David Gordon (1978), perhaps because, as John La Valle's article of November 08, 2016, (PureNLP.com) points out, "NLP is not therapy. Period!" It gives us a interesting look at the relationship NLP has to psychotherapy. He goes on to say, "If NLP is NOT Therapy, then what is it? NLP is a meta discipline, that is, it is a discipline of disciplines. It is the study of the structure of subjective experience and what can be calculated from that. The greatest misconception about the technology is that it is about therapy and that is about as far from the truth as one can get!"

I remember asking a colleague who heard that I was doing research on therapeutic metaphors, what she thought of Gordon's book, *Therapeutic Metaphors*. The clinician said that she had

---

* Milton H. Erickson died in March, 1980, "leaving a lasting legacy to the worlds of psychology, psychiatry, psychotherapy, hypnotherapy, pedagogics and communications." (https://en.wikipedia.org/wiki/Milton_H._Erickson.)

approached the book with great enthusiasm expecting that she would finally learn something useful about a tool she felt potentially important to her work. She said she was sorely disappointed that she had to put the book down soon after she started it, and that she felt stupid (having no idea of the fundamentals of NLP, notably Gordon's use of calibrations, sub-personalities, sub-modalities, anchors and triggers, etc.), not being able to follow his extensive presentation. I asked her what she knew about Neurolinguistic Programming (NLP). She replied, "I received a whole lot of flyers in the mail announcing their seminars!"

In her Introduction to *Practical Magic*, Leslie Cameron-Bandler states, "NLP is so alien to psychotherapy that only a psychotherapist of Steve Lankton's caliber could have exacted the essential fundamentals for making such a meaningful translation" (Lankton, 1980, p. 4). Perhaps it also takes a psychotherapist of "Lankton's caliber" to understand and glean something from NLP's approach to metaphor.

What is needed, then, is a clear and understandable explanation and guide for the use and construction of the extended metaphor in the psychotherapeutic process. The following is my attempt to "plug-in" the therapeutic metaphor to the context and structure of the more dynamic paradigm of psychotherapy. It is my belief that this broader formulation will accommodate the uniqueness of most clinicians' working style, as well as preserving spontaneity. This proposed model will elucidate the fundamental principles of therapeutic change that can be facilitated by this valuable technique of therapy.

As a clinician working with this model, you will employ therapeutic techniques to help the client, (a) become aware of the sources of stress and conflict, (b) recognize unproductive behaviors and their consequences, (c) confront unacceptable parts of the personality, and (d) understand the origins of maladaptive repetitive patterns.

It is generally accepted in this paradigm that much of the turmoil that clients experience is at an unconscious level and that the defense mechanisms of repression and denial (among a variety of resistances) operate to ward off the anxiety that would be released if this turmoil were allowed to rise to the level of awareness. Awareness and insight can enable the client to better develop more productive and rewarding patterns of behavior, to free himself or herself from old values, lead toward a more realistic concept of self that can result in security, self–fulfillment, and self-esteem.

4   The Metaphorical Framework

Metaphor refers to the process of helping the client to identify a different framework for understanding and responding to a problem.
—Lankton, *Practical Magic*

Metaphor especially has clarity and sweetness and strangeness.
—Aristotle, *The Rhetoric*

A metaphor consists of the projection of one schema (the source domain of the metaphor) onto another schema (the target domain of the metaphor).
—Karen S. Moser, "Metaphor Analysis in Psychology"

SOME OF THE PRINCIPLES that provide the framework for the extended metaphor are common to the process of all modalities of psychotherapy, and I will describe them here. Although my orientation is dynamic, and the information I am supplying here reflects my clinical approach and experience, clinicians of all modalities can benefit from my overall message.

First, however, keep in mind that, for the most part, research articles in psychology are written by a small coterie of writers who have been deeply impassioned by the subject matter and address each other's prejudices and idiosyncrasies colloquially. This appears to alienate clinicians who are put off by this elite camp and thus feel encouraged to seek out more concrete modes of inquiry. The work of Milton H. Erickson and his followers, as well as that of the Neurolinguistic Programmers, constitute worthwhile contributions, but these contributions are too specific and narrow to meet the needs of most mental health practitioners. Saying this, I believe that a more universal approach is even more important today. A glaring omission from the literature is a broader formulation of the use of therapeutic metaphor to accommodate the various psychotherapeutic styles. I intend to meet that need here.

The principles that follow are the pegs on which to hang your metaphorical hat; they are the background or framework that best encompasses this important tool of therapy. It is a wider berth than what is allowable in the existing orientations. It is fitted to a collection of principles that illustrate the function and use of the extended psychotherapeutic metaphor I am proposing. When seen against this specific background and tied to this definite set of dynamic principles, you can achieve the understanding needed to construct and utilize metaphors effectively.

The principles that best describe the therapeutic metaphor follow the design of the therapy process itself. All the elements or ingredients that form a metaphor are found in the work of a clinician. No matter your theoretical orientation, as a general rule the following procedures are essential to the conduct of psychotherapy: (a) establishing a working therapeutic relationship, (b) determining the problem and defining goals, and (c) dealing with resistance to change.

Establishing a Working Therapeutic Relationship

Without those basic ingredients there can be no hope for a successful therapeutic outcome. I will therefore spend some additional time on those objectives. Your relationship with your client may be said to be the first objective and perhaps the most unstructured. A few formal techniques (the metaphor may be among the most effective) can be used to engender trust, gain the client's confidence, give the client a feeling of support, and stimulate the client's motivation and sense of hope. Many describe the working relationship as the most important "ally" to help the client achieve his or her goals of therapy.

In this respect, therapeutic metaphors serve as a vehicle to create closeness or intimacy between teller and listener, between clinician and client. In the normal course of therapy you try to produce and maintain an empathetic response to the feeling state of your client. This can achieve the needed closeness and create the intimacy necessary to work with him or her. In the case whereby you are finding difficulty with the client who is not able to attune himself with his feelings, who may find embarrassment when focusing on feelings, or requires an inordinate amount of time to share feelings with you, the metaphor will be extremely useful. The therapeutic metaphor can also establishes empathetic rapport with the client's unconscious. It is a way to bypass many of the sensory mechanism the client uses to protect against betrayal of trust and perceived rejection, by appealing to the deeper levels of the client's psyche along with ongoing empathetic behavior on your part.

Ted Cohen (1976) discusses the aspect of metaphor he calls "achievement of intimacy." Such intimacy involves how the two participants, clinician and client, experience a shared feeling to which only they are privileged. It can be likened to a shared experience of "giving" and "receiving," which creates a unique bond as the two are drawn closer to one another. This can be illustrated as (a) the speaker issuing a kind of concealed invitation, (b) the hearer making a special effort to accept the invitation, and (c) the transaction constituting the acknowledgment of community. Although one may argue that the transaction also takes place in ordinary literal discourse, the use of the metaphor throws it into relief. Here's an example to illustrate the concept. In the early stages of therapy, you might tell your client an anecdote about how a friend became initiated into the teaching profession, a story about your friend's experience as a neophyte teacher in an area with one of the highest crime rates in the city.

> I'd like to tell you about a friend of mine, Mitch, whose beginning teaching days also put him in a new and unfamiliar situation. It was more than a little scary for Mitch to be faced with problems he wasn't sure he could deal with. He was placed in a sixth grade class in

a school in one of the highest crime areas of the city, and taking care of himself wasn't his strong suit. He was even more concerned with how he would take care of those children put in his charge. He admitted that the fear of failing to be the kind of teacher he wanted to be was truly the greater problem.

Mitch remembers standing in front of 35 fifth-grade, poverty level "wise guys," kids whose main function in life (he perceived at the time) was to tear his head off. Mitch dealt with their constant verbal and physical fighting, as he made feeble attempts to teach reading and math to kids whose proficiency levels ranged from first grade to fifth grade. Mitch was really feeling sorry for himself and maybe with good cause! For the entire first month not a soul stepped forth to lend a hand. Mitch's assistant principal, Mr. Conrad, was friendly enough. He always smiled as he hurried past in the hall and yelled," How's things going, Mitch?" Mitch always managed to muster up a grin and mumble something like, "Okay, thanks." It got so bad that he finally took steps to help himself: Mitch made an appointment to see Mr. Conrad in his office after his class let out. Now for Mitch this was a major decision. He was, quite frankly, more anxious dealing with Mr. Conrad than dealing with the kids. He somehow felt that asking for special help was the equivalent to admitting that he couldn't hack it as a teacher. Such an admission was completely unacceptable, even unbearable to him, because he truly loved those kids and wanted more than anything to be a good teacher—maybe an outstanding one. He believed that his pride was preventing him from facing what he perceived as his inadequacy to do so vital a job. Mitch wasn't sure he was ready to face himself then, either, but he knew he had to do something. He walked to Mr. Conrad's office waiting for the ax to fall.

Then a strange thing happened. Mr. Conrad turned on one of his knowing smiles, one that made Mitch feel that the assistant principal pretty much understood the turmoil that was happening inside of him. Mitch was filled with relief when Mr. Conrad said, "Goodness, I'm so glad you finally came in to talk. I was getting worried that I would have to make the appointment to see you. It's important, Mitch, that you feel ready to ask for help yourself; it will make a major difference in how much assistance you will be able to accept from me. With your permission, then, let's get started!"

The client may have been taken by surprise by the clinician's story about his friends teaching days, unable to account for the reason for such a story at the time. It is obvious that something is also "behind" the clinician's story, something he wants the client to understand. Once the client realizes he is offered a metaphor, he is required to "unpack" it to understand what is really being sent to him. A transaction is the setup in which the clinician and client actively engage each other in a communicative process at various levels. The client must "penetrate" the meaning in order to understand the clinician's intent, for the meaning is not on the surface of the communication. An implicit understanding exists: both parties have consented to participate in the transaction. The client becomes acutely aware that something is transpiring outside the normal communication pattern and enters into the agreement. The clinician has invited him in. Certain requirements have been set up. The client takes up the requirements and the two achieve a degree of intimacy that does not occur in ordinary literal discourse. It is clear that a mutually active process is taking place both in the speaker (the clinician conveying an intentional message in the form of a metaphor) and the listener (the client taking up the invitation to discover that message). It is the "nod of recognition," the sudden burst of laughter when one "gets it," the "Aha" of discovery that constitutes the sound of shared intimacy. It is, more so, the sharing of the intimate idea through a figurative mode of expression that is so singular that only the community of two can fully understand and appreciate its richness. The therapeutic metaphor can be the source of that richness as it acts as a device to foster the working relationships between clinician and client.

It would be fair to say that many clients who enter therapy for the first time have no clear idea about what they are about to undertake. Others have inaccurate expectations, which can hinder their progress. The following metaphor can be used to help a client better understand the role of the clinician and the responsibilities of the client:

> I've found that a good way to explain the therapy pro-
> cess is to compare it to buying a pair of shoes: a fine
> pair of shoes, that is! When you walk into a fine shoe
> shop you are immediately aware of so many pairs of
> shoes to choose from that you may initially be discour-
> aged, thinking that you'll never find the right ones for
> you. That's where a good sales person comes in. (Use
> the gender of the therapist here) He will make you feel
> comfortable and assure you that the objective is to help
> you find just what you require after first helping you to
> know and describe just what it is you are looking for.
> Many times you don't have a clear idea what it is that
> you'll be most happy with. His job, then, is to help you
> choose what is just right for you by helping you, narrow
> down the kind of shoes you would like for yourself. Are
> you looking for formal footwear, or something casual?
> Will it be open at the front? A boot, perhaps? Brown,
> black . . . red? A good shoe salesperson can really help
> you decide what's right for you.
>
> He may bring you several pair based on your
> initial requirements, after sizing you up, so to speak!
> Using his knowledge of the inventory and his expe-
> rience, several alternatives are presented for you to
> try on. Once a pair of shoes has been carefully fitted
> to your feet, you may stand up and walk around to
> see how they feel. Are they comfortable? A little too
> tight? Which ones feel good and which just don't fit!
> He would never presume to know how the shoes
> feel to you; it is your choice, your responsibility to
> choose the right one. He may tell you how they look
> to an observer, may provide information on how

they are made, may even describe personal experi- ence with similar choices. After you walk in them for a little while, you may decide that you need to reconsider. Perhaps they really don't fit as well as you first thought. Perhaps a different choice would be more appropriate, even better. But the choice is always yours. And if you pay close attention to this process, you will likely find what you are looking for.

Determining the Problem and Defining Goals

The therapeutic metaphor can be conceptualized as an interven- tion employed by the clinician to aid the client to achieve the goals of therapy. The client may formulate the goals in broad terms: for example, "I want to control my temper with my spouse." It is not unusual for clients to "mis-take" their situations and be un- able to see past the presenting problem that brought them into the clinician's office. Clinicians of all working modalities must find the sources of the problem that is interfering with the client's adjustment. They pay ample attention to environmental stresses and distortions in interpersonal relationships, as well as learned patterns that lead to destructive behavior. The clinician using the dynamic model to accomplish problem resolution and reconstruc- tive change, will pay special attention to helping the client bring to consciousness the dynamic turmoil going on below the level of consciousness. That way, the clinician helps the client become aware of what is happening to her at this unconscious level.

It is fair to say that many clients enter therapy in a confused, bewildered, and even at times, an extremely painful state. Her symptoms seem to be experienced apart from what she believes about herself. "I can't believe this is really happening to me," or "This isn't really me!" are common statements about some of her own negative behaviors and their consequences. Unaware that some presenting symptoms stem from the deep conflicts that may originate from her early life events, she cannot make sense of the present disturbances in her personal goals and relationships with others. In order to make progress, the client must become aware that her symptoms, in the form of her current dysfunctional behavior, are not always independent manifestations of present circumstances. They may, instead, be manifestations of repetitive patterns of which she has little recognition. These unconscious motivations have become incorporated into the self and promote actions that inhibit productive living.

It is the clinician's task to help the client recognize and understand the underlying dynamics that may be influencing the client's feelings and activities. To construct an effective therapeutic metaphor—or for that matter, to make any worthwhile intervention—it is taken for granted that the clinician will know the client's history and determine the presenting problem facing the client. I would, however, wish to share with you an aspect of the problem's boundaries with Fritz Perls' (1969, p. 291) well-known warning, "A good therapist doesn't listen to the content of the bullshit the patient produces," meaning (perhaps metaphorically) that the clinician need always be vigilant concerning what the client says in terms of "telling the truth." Although some clients consciously lie directly to clinicians to accomplish their goal, others may be unable to tell the truth to themselves through the person of the clinician. Several other issues of "accuracy" are embodied in the therapeutic relationship itself between the clinician and client. A client may have an underlying anxiety about revealing "too much too soon" to the clinician, thinking, "Will I really be understood and not judged for my behavior?" It is a risk a client may yet be unable to take. Recognition of the truth of the situation may be tainted or even contaminated not simply by these special conditions but inherent in the therapeutic relationship. As a result, the client learns how to gain approval, get attention, and at times, "strike back" at the clinician by giving the kind of information the client believes will accomplish these ends.

In the Family Therapy paradigm, a number of smoke screens permeate the therapy process that can inhibit the client's ability to see beyond a presenting problem. A child may be designated the identified patient, and the clinician is asked to "fix" a child who is actually acting out the pain of the family system's pathology. Scapegoating is a mutual causal process, not simply one in which one member is victimized. All members, including the scapegoat, participate in the process. By displacing their conflicts onto a child, parents frequently maintain harmonious relationships at the expense of the child's emotional development. The child, in turn, may be struggling to keep the family intact, even if the child is sacrificing himself or herself.

The following example illustrates a possible use of metaphor that accommodates the above barrier to accurately address the family problem situation. A couple came to see me because they felt that their 14-year-old daughter was extremely immature and did very little taking care of herself. After several visits with the entire family, I assessed both parents as overprotective of their daughter to the point of fostering dependency. As part of my treatment plan I related the following extended metaphor to introduce the possibility to the family.

> When I first moved into my house there was a young tree in the backyard. Admittedly, I'm not an expert on trees, but it was apparent that's something was wrong with the tree. It was undersized, quite stunted in its growth. It had a few leaves, certainly fewer than healthy trees its age. When I approached it closer I realized that it was straddled by two low iron bars driven into the ground. The tree was bound tightly to them by heavy rope. They had evidently been place there to support the young tree during the first years of growth.
>
> Well, the first thing I did was to cut the rope and remove the bars. At first the young tree bent almost to the ground. This might be expected when we think that it was always supported from the outside. It was not receiving enough of the natural nourishment a young growing tree would need: sunlight and water. I gave it some extra water during the first few months it was on its own. The tree responded well to its new freedom and before long it grew straight and strong. It used its inner resources to compensate for those objects outside of itself that held

it up. It now supports itself and has a large number of leaves and a straight trunk. I'm pleased to share its shade and beauty.

—Based on a metaphor provided by Charles Kuell, PhD

Dealing with Resistance to Change

In the course of therapy, a client can discover that her symptoms are not isolated occurrences but are triggered by a specific set of circumstances involving current attitudes toward others and the self. Many of the attitudes are derived from, and hook into, long-standing unconscious forces that infringe upon her freedom of behavior. This discovery process may be a long and complex affair. She will be faced with great difficulties in procuring therapeutic change due to a stunted ability to recognize negative aspects of her personality. She may experience her values and character traits as anything but acceptable to her fragile ego, and that her attitudes and fears may not be a product of something other than her current interactions. The client may resist facing inner conflicts that may generate intense emotions and anxieties. She may find it too uncomfortable to accept the irrationality of some of her behaviors and their accompanying emotions. To help the client deal with her resistance to exploring these difficulties, the clinician uses such interviewing techniques as accenting, summarizing, restating, extending support, and establishing connections (see any basic text on the techniques of psychotherapy for a full account of the interviewing process). Making interpretations is generally held as the cornerstone of the interviewing process. The clinician may also explore with the client unconscious material through dreams and fantasies.

Although the means by which a client is helped to awareness of present conflicts depends on the theoretical orientation in which you have been trained, an important focus of every psychodynamic model is to bring unconscious material to conscious awareness. Doing so exposes the client's unconscious conflicts.

Once this process is under way, once the repressed material begins to be uncovered, anxiety will appear and stimulate the client's defense mechanisms. The function of the resistance will be to keep intact those mechanisms that are co-working to deal with the perceived danger to the client's psyche. Basic adaptational patterns that constituted the client's personality are now asked to be viewed as unacceptable, and the client's way of being is challenged. The neurotic symptoms that brought him to therapy have also served to protect his ego functioning, and the therapeutic process is asking that hidden or secondary gains be forfeited. It would seem fitting that the client would resort to behaviors that head off such a stripping bare of the ego. He may feel discouraged, helpless to change, hopeless or hostile, listless, bored, irritable and accusatory toward the clinician that he isn't being understood. He may "forget" therapy appointments or develop a "flight into health."

To combat this resistance, the clinician's most effective tool, according to Lankton and Lankton (1983, p. 159), is interpretation—or what is termed "direct suggestion." Direct suggestion can facilitate rapid change when a client knows exactly what change is desired, is congruent about wanting that outcome, and has the necessary resources available and aligned so as to produce that outcome. Obviously, this is a hypothetical situation, which rarely occurs in a therapy session. The use of indirect suggestion as a device to help create self-motivation in clients is, therefore, paramount.

Motivating a person to act, to adopt new behaviors, is more difficult than engendering a more constructive attitude in the client. To get behavior change you must consider many factors, among them your status as clinician/storyteller in your client's eyes, how your client views the consequences of his new behavior, social pressure to change (or not change), and his coping skills to handle the change. Lankton and Lankton (1983, p. 83) conclude: "Increased resistance or increased motivation can result as clients hear a new metaphoric framework detailed."

If all the pieces are in place, the clinician can then point out to the client that what he is doing is resistant to his goals of change and, perhaps, why he is resisting. This interpretive process promotes insight by attacking barriers to confronting anxiety. The client's defenses against anxiety may force him to react in irrational and inappropriate ways to persons and events. When the anxiety is confronted, the client begins to understand the origins of these emotions and how his defenses put up blocks to ward them off.

The most effective use of interpretation takes place when the client is led to make his own interpretation. This can be achieved through the interviewing technique in such a way that the client can gather the cues and use his sequences of the material that was skillfully arranged by the clinician. The client then discovers for himself and incorporates his insights into his quest for change. It is also possible that a client's resistance will be greater than what most interviewing techniques can accommodate; then a clinician's direct interpretation will be necessary to move the process forward. If the therapeutic relationship is strong, and the clinician presents the interpretation in a nonjudgmental way, with the client's "necessary resources available and aligned," and with the client feeling free to reject it, then the effect can be positive. The clinician will have ample opportunities for direct interpretations when the client's resistance prevents him from making his own, and the appropriate sets of criteria are in motion. It is also true however, that this approach may lead to negative results. One can imagine a client experiencing this kind of directness as an attack that demands even greater fortification against increased anxiety. This in turn may produce increased resistance toward the warded-off unconscious material.

It is at this point that you can see the potential value of the therapeutic metaphor to the therapy process. You can view the metaphor as an intervention that can accomplish what may not be accomplished through the use of direct interpretation. You can conceptualize the therapeutic metaphor as an "indirect interpretation" you can use to deal with the client's resistance so as to foster insight. It will be most appropriate in a case where the client cannot consciously confront a painful task, for example, the loss of a personal loving relationship or the realization of hatred of a family member. These problems may appear as something quite intolerable and unacceptable to have to incorporate into the self. The clinician, working with a client who is striving to maintain psychic homeostasis, will be met with an ample amount of resistance to reject insight concerning his problem. The following metaphor can be employed to help a client confront such unconscious material and enable insight to become consciously acceptable. It is a particularly good example of the capacity of a therapeutic metaphor to indirectly confront consciously painful and unacceptable material.

The case involves a 19-year-old female client living with her mother and father. She had recently brought to awareness a previously repressed memory of being sexually abused by her father when she was a child. She had great resistance to dealing further with her frightening "discovery." To break through the resistance, her clinician told the following story about a former client who had experienced a devastating earthquake that destroyed her home:

> There was a young woman I treated a few years ago who had undergone a terrible experience. She was caught in an earthquake that virtually destroyed her home and whose violence shook the very foundation of her being. As she stood in the aftermath of the destruction, she felt as if the whole structure of her life had collapsed to the ground; not a support left standing! She was so bewildered by the rubble, so overwhelmed by the debris everywhere, that she wanted to run away and pretend that the earthquake had not happened. She felt violated . . . the victim of a violent act.
>
> The young woman, feeling that her world had tumbled down around her, sought help. She contacted an architect who was recommended to her on the basis of his experience with similar circumstances. He talk to her as if he really understood the shock and grief she was feeling and she began to feel a little more hopeful that she would be in greater control of her life. He suggested that she could reconstruct her home in such a way that it would be strong and secure, that she could be at peace living within its basic structure. He pointed out, however, that it would be necessary not only to clear away the old debris, but also to carefully examine the

structural weaknesses and strengths where they existed. This extremely difficult and somewhat exhausting task would be needed to create a new, safer, and more secure structure. Perhaps she will discover that things were not constructed the way she thought they were, that problems previously unattended to led to the breakdown of her former home.

At first she recoiled against having to deal with this emotionally painful situation. Slowly she began to accept the architect's advice that she needed to understand what had happened to cause such turmoil in her life before she could effectively make the needed changes to create a new home. Soon she found herself sifting through the ruins of her former house with the enthusiasm that comes from a heartfelt belief that she was doing the right thing for herself. She became more and more hopeful and gained the confidence that she would find the kind of answers that would allow her to get on with the rebuilding her life.

—Based on a metaphor provided by to Karen Michael Peoples, PhD

By hearing an anecdote that refers to objects or events that, on the surface, are enough dissimilar to her own circumstances, the client was more willing to enter the "the area of anxiety." To this point, Paivio and Walsh (Ortony, 1979, p. 309) state that "the incongruity of metaphor induces arousal, which the person seeks to reduce by means of a 'conceptual resolution' of the disparate elements." The client, then, is highly motivated to search and translate these "disparate elements" of the metaphor into his or her own problem situation. To engage the attention of the client, the metaphor must contain similar important elements and relationships as those in the client's problem. In many cases, the meaning of the intervention may not be consciously understood immediately, but grasped at the unconscious level. It may take a client time to sort through his files of life experiences that coincide with the action presented in the metaphor and bring to the surface his underlying problem. An extended metaphor can be viewed as a kind of puzzle, whose meaning triggers memory or information in the client that is associated with elements presented in the metaphor, which the client then applies to his own situation. I call these elements "retrieval cues" that are mediated by what the client "gets" from hearing the metaphor.

A therapeutic metaphor is decidedly less threatening than direct interpretation as a form of intervention. Metaphors are special or singular communication devices that express meaning in a way that cannot be reproduced or duplicated in a literal or direct form. They convey meaning or a message with the particular impact that is inherent in its form and structure. It can be compared to the experience of being at the theater to see the performance of a play, as opposed to reading its text. Their qualitative difference makes each experience unique, and unduplicated, although the "messages" are the same. The therapeutic metaphor, in its uniqueness of form, encourages the removal of repression, the stirring up of unconscious material, and the fostering of insight because it does something different from direct interpretation. It presents a message to a client in a way that cannot be achieved by direct or literal statement. Metaphors evoke a fresh and novel examination of an issue that is possible in no other way (as Marshall McLuhan pointed out: "The medium is the message."). Commenting on a case where he used an extended metaphor and obtained a successful result, Lankton (1980, p. 161) says, "Knowing that a treatment metaphor is just that—a story designed to help expand the clients own story—sets us free to use any metaphor that is appropriate and to even make up stories that are specifically suited to the client's needs." He goes on to comment on the successful outcome. "The story had apparently initiated mental searches, associations and meaning of this man's dilemma and had let him use his own experiences to guide his readiness for the rest of the therapy session" (1980, p. 167). Let us not forget, however, that a therapeutic metaphor is never complete in itself. The parable, teaching story, or anecdote has unshared or individualistic characteristics that cannot be captured by a direct statement of an issue. It's not intended to meet all the needs of the client in its telling, but it is a valuable tool, one of many interventions that will help ease the client into a pattern of positive change.

5   A Model for Original Metaphor Construction

Metaphor is the omnipresent principle of all language.
—I. A. Richards, *Practical Criticism*

Whole works of scientific research, even entire schools, are hardly
more than the patient repetition, in all its ramifications, of the first
tile metaphor.
—Kenneth Burke, *A Grammar of Motives*

The most profound social creativity consists in the invention and
imposition of new, radical metaphors.
—R. Kaufman, in Murry, *Countries of the Mind*

WE BEGIN WITH AN overview of the metaphor construction process,
and then explain each stage of construction, and provide several
examples of therapeutic metaphors. Two full case studies of hypothetical clients are also presented, which includes the components
outlined here to help you understand how each particular component contributes to the effectiveness of a therapeutic metaphor.

Laying the Groundwork begins with knowing your client. Clinicians have their individual ways of determining and document-
ing a client's family history, the problem and its manifestations,
environmental disturbances, relationships, and level of insight and
motivation. Next comes determining the Purpose of Intervention,
which involves establishing rapport, creating intimacy, and dealing with resistance.

Creating the Basic Metaphor involves deciding which of the available Forms is most likely to work for a client: allegory, anecdote, fable, fairy tale, etc. You will need to engage the client's comfort level by choosing an appropriate level of language. Then you need to decide on the tone (serious? humorous?), the degree of realism, the interest categories (hobbies? sports?) likely to engage the client's interest. When you have picked a Form and Style that encompass tone, the degree of realism, and interest categories, you can begin to set up characters, time and place, and the sequence of events that result in a successful outcome.

I will spend additional time to explain how to choose the correct Enhancements such as points of correspondence, embedded suggestions, and positive expectations that will facilitate reaching successful outcomes.

Laying the Groundwork

Know your client

You, as a clinician, are perfectly capable of accomplishing this process using your own procedures to collect this data and will be familiar with your client's (a) current manifestations: symptoms, attitudes, and behaviors; (b) environmental disturbances: work, economy, family, housing; (c) relationships with significant others and attitude toward self; and (d) level of insight and motivation.

Purpose of Intervention

To choose the most appropriate form of metaphor to present to your client, you must first decide what you wish for your intervention to accomplish. If the client were having difficulty "opening up" and revealing information about himself, you would present a metaphor aimed at establishing greater rapport between yourself and your client. If the client is, for example, unable to overcome feelings of hopelessness, the aim of the intervention can be to reframe or redefine a seemingly "hopeless" situation and increase the client's motivation to improve and change.

Many choices of metaphors are available to aid in fostering trust, or you can design your own to this end.

Let us suppose your client has told you that he wants to improve his marriage and he's pointed out many things his wife has done that he believes are threats to the marriage. He asked for suggestions to change her behavior, indicating that it is she, not he, who needs to change. Here is a sample metaphor for such a situation.

> I'd like you to listen to what was written in a letter to me. When I was young and free my imagination had no limits, I dreamed of changing the world. As I grew older and wiser I discovered the world would not change. So I shortened my sights somewhat and decided to change only my country. But it, too, seemed immovable. As I grew into my twilight years, in one last desperate attempt, I settled for changing only my family, those closest to me. But, alas, they would have none of it. And now, that I'm older and wiser, I suddenly realize, if I had only changed, myself first, then, by example, I would have changed my family. From their inspiration and encouragement, I would have then been able to better my country and who knows, I may have even changed the world.
>
> —Based on an inscription from the tomb of a Bishop in Westminster Abbey 1100 AD.*

---

* Kopp (1971) relates Martin Buber's understanding of problems that arise between people in terms of "each man must begin with himself." He goes on to say, "A man is not merely an object to be examined, with problems to be analyzed away, but a person who is upon to 'straightened himself out.' Rather than simply blaming the other person with whom he is struggling, he must take on the difficult responsibility of turning his attention to his own part in this, with no more then the hope that the other will do the same for himself. One way of stating this in Hasidic terms would be: the origin of the conflicts which I experience between myself and others is to be found in the fact that too often I do not know what I feel, I do not say what I mean, and I do not do what I say. It is in large part a matter of being honest with myself. Everything depends on myself and only I can straighten myself out."

Lloyd, a young man of 20, complained that he was disappointed with the choice of a new girlfriend. "I like her and all," he said, "but she turned out not to be what I thought she was." I related the following story:

> I was once accompanying a friend on a long trip. Shortly on the way, I took and peeled a round fruit. I offered my friend a portion to share with me. He longingly bit into the wedge, but grimaced with sharp annoyance.
> "This is a terrible orange," he finally blurted out.
> "That's not an orange," I retorted, "It's a grapefruit!"
> Recovering, he took another bite and said happily," what a perfectly fine grapefruit."
> The tree of life is also filled with grapefruit. If you are set for oranges, you will always be disappointed.
> —Based on a metaphor by Peter N. Alevizos, PhD

The Basic Metaphor

Form

There are many forms in which to present a metaphor. Although each form traditionally has been directed toward a specific end, whether to minimize the seriousness of a situation, or to teach a moral lesson, any direct message addressing the client's dilemma can be transported through many different metaphorical forms. When I speak of presenting a metaphor either in an existing form (the Biblical parables or a fable from Aesop's Fables), which can be delivered just as it is written, or one that is constructed by you as an anecdote or designed like a parable or fable etc., we are talking about a story. It can simply be thought of as a story, as is Erickson's "Teaching Story", that can take many different forms. It would be up to your discretion to choose the form of metaphor that best fits your client.

Once you are familiar with your client's history and presenting problem, and have determined the purpose for your intervention, you can decide on the form your metaphor will take. You might choose a pre-existing form and deliver it as is, or adjust it as to conform to your client's requirements while leaving the metaphor's basic structure intact. Another choice is to create a new metaphor using one of the previously mentioned metaphorical forms, such as an allegory or anecdote.

When choosing a Zen lesson for one client, I considered his intellectual level and interests. Thomas was a young man in his mid-twenties, who described himself as a "spiritual" person and continually complained about his boss, who overlooked him for a promotion. He had filed a grievance about the situation more than six months before, but was ruled against. At this, he said he wasn't surprised, "I've had bad luck all my life. Nothing seems to go my way." As a result he thought about quitting his job and "traveling around for a while back home" in rural Montana.

Thomas, it appeared, had outstanding abilities, but held onto his grievances to the point of doing poorly at work and in his private life. He had relationship problems with a woman friend, and other past problems he was unwilling to deal with. Holding on to his past hurts and resentments was preventing Thomas from living in the present and finding peace and fulfillment. Here is a Zen lesson I chose for him.

> This is a story about a young man of 25, who, having faced great difficulties in his life believed he could escape them by joining a monastery and living the celibate life of a monk. He often sought guidance from an older monk who had experienced similar difficulties and was willing to share his wisdom with him.
>
> The young monk took many journeys into the mountains to find solitude and inner peace. But on this day he felt compelled to ask the older monk to accompany him. Agreeing, both set out across the difficult terrain. Not far into the journey they came across a young woman sitting by the side of a fast moving stream. She told them that she had fallen from her horse and twisted her ankle. Unable to walk she asked for their assistance to cross the stream to reach her horse grazing on the other side.

The woman said she had been waiting a long time for help and must mount her horse quickly so that she could return to her home safely before it became dark. The young monk tried to explain to her that he was observant and that his vow of chastity forbade him from touching a woman. He was torn when he thought of the danger the young woman could face alone in the night, but could not approach her.

At that moment the older monk reached down and lifted the young woman into his arms and carried her across the stream and placed her on her horse so that she could resume her safe journey home. With that, the two monks continued their journey through the mountains.

After walking a short time, the young monk became more and more agitated at what he witnessed from the older monk. It got to the point where he could not restrain himself, and he exclaimed, "How could you do such a thing? You have broken your vow of chastity by touching that woman with your body?" The older monk turned to him, and with a confident smile replied, "Yes, it's true I carried her in my arms, but I put her down on the other side of the stream. It seems, my young brother, you are still carrying her."

—Based on "Two Monks and a Woman—A Zen Lesson"

Theme Qualities

The theme, the dominating circumstances of the story action that motivates the character's behavior, is shaped by three elements of metaphor construction.

Style and tone

First consider the style, such qualities as serious, humorous, and its position on a realism spectrum. As you decide upon the form your metaphor will take, you will take into account the serious or humorous nature of the client's problem. Of course, you also consider the nature of the client. Then you determine how likely the client is to respond well to a light or serious approach. When considering the degree of realism to use, consider that some clients may feel uncomfortable if you tell them a fairytale and some respond best to jokes or satirical stories.

Interest Categories

To address the second theme element, note a client's hobbies, things he likes to do, places he has enjoyed visiting, events that interest him, for example, sports, opera, or acting. The objective here is to present a metaphoric theme that the client is likely to be comfortable with. It would obviously be more effective to present a client who is a gardener by trade with a metaphor about the growth of plants and trees, whereas a story about a sailboat race would fall flat with a client who had never sailed and doesn't know a jib from a buoy!

Language

Finally, you will choose the level of vocabulary to use in your metaphor considering the client's level of formal education or natural intelligence and self-education. A college-educated client requires a level of language befitting his education, even if the metaphor you present is in the form of a fairytale. This, of course, holds true in all verbal discourse you conduct with a client, but it's worth including here to guard against talking down—or "up"—to a client when your message is in the form of a device, like a fairytale, usually reserved for children.

Language also involves vocabulary that can be identified with a specific area of life. For a person steeped in a business career and heavily involved with finance issues, the pattern may include words and phrases like, "Would you be willing to save the relationship?" "It sounds like a bankrupt situation." "Do you think he's worth investing in?" The pattern for a person who is a compulsive gambler may include, "It's a horse race." "We're coming into the home stretch." "Sounds like she's betting on you."

It is clear that language is a critical theme quality element because it provides your client with an appropriate comfort level in the way the subject is presented, and provides identifiable features for the client to tie into.

Properties of Construction

Building the metaphor is accomplished in three stages: (a) it begins with setting up the structural elements of the story, such as place and time; (b) the middle shows the unfolding events, how the character gets from one emotional place to another; and (c) the resolution, in which the story's character reaches a successful outcome.

The Set-Up

The structural elements of this first stage are (a) who, the characters to populate the metaphor; (b) where, the place the action is located; (c) the setting that describes what is happening in the story and speaks to the common life experiences of the client; (d) the time the metaphorical events are occurring. When well chosen, these elements supply the next stage, "Getting There," with a framework to accommodate the events as they unfold in the story.

Getting There

The second stage in building the metaphor story line involves the movement of events. It tells what happens to the character you intend the client to identify with. There must be enough similarities between what happens to the story character and what the client has experienced to create a feeling of commonality. This point of resemblance offers similarity in a sea of difference. The story must have enough similarity, features shared by both, yet at the same time, have enough differences that the client can sufficiently distance himself from the impact of a direct assault to his senses. A client may identify fully with either a rabbit or turtle in a race, to a poor stepchild who is sought after by a charming prince, or a story character that serves as both a model for the client's situation and the emotional state the client is striving to achieve. The degree of such similarities is also discussed in the section on Points of Correspondence.

Resolution

To complete your metaphor, conceive of a resolution to the story character's dilemma. To preface this section I offer a cautionary note by quoting from Robert Resnick's article, "Chicken Soup is Poison" (1978, p. 142).

> In order to make chicken soup, you have to kill a chicken. Although not particularly leading to self-actualization for the chicken, this sacrifices the bird to a greater cause—being helpful. Combined with onions, greens, carrots, water and seasoning, the resulting elixir is ready for its role as a helper. The giving of chicken soup is an attempt to help the other, to do for him, to make him feel better. The chubby, sponge-like matzo ball, not un-like the unconscious, lies 90% below the surface of the soup. By the time the unaware gourmet has had enough of this brew, the soup around the submerged matzo ball has cooled and, like a dead submarine, it spews forth its fatty oil slick. CAUTION: chicken soup is likely to be as fatal to the recipient as it was to the contributing poultry.

Metaphors in themselves, offer no solutions. The solution to a client's problem is not contained solely in the content of the metaphor. Nor do you, as a clinician, offer the solution to a client's problem, whether in a direct interpretation or indirectly in the body of a metaphor. Resnick (1975, p. 145) says it well:

> The most popular way therapists "help" their patients to avoid standing on their own is to first deny that they have the blueprints and answers the patient is asking for.

(Of course, the therapist doesn't believe this.) This done, the therapist "helps" the patient with the content of his problems (e.g., he manipulates the patient into discovering for himself what the therapist knew all the time). Even if I assume (and I do not) that the clinician is better equipped to make decisions than the patient himself, I am convinced that this leaves the patient no better off than when he started. If anything, he is a worse cripple. The lyrics of his problem to change over the months and years, but the melody lingers on and on.

The client must own up to his part that created the problem in the first place. The others he blames for his being weak or insecure, for example, are not his problem; blaming others is! Acting the victim and holding others responsible for who he is today is a function of his non-awareness of the fact that blaming others stands as a barrier to his growth. As Resnick (1975, p. 146) so aptly concludes, "When he is in touch with his responsibility, his ability to respond, he enters a world of possibilities, choices and freedom. As long as he blames the other, he remains impotent."

In terms of behavior change, the metaphor can be thought of as the "how," the vehicle to deliver the possibilities while the client reserves the choice and freedom to help himself change. The client has the ultimate responsibility to solve his problem. Using the indirectness of a metaphor, you can give support by offering hope, positive expectations, motivating ideas, and an alternative and novel way of approaching a difficult problem. Because the situation portrayed in the metaphor only parallels the client's true situation, the metaphor's identifiable circumstances and its positive outcome, serves to motivate the client to search his own experiences and ideas to confront his present difficulties. Never present—or intend to present—a direct solution, no matter how cleverly cloaked in metaphorical garb. The story resolution is what may be termed a "successful outcome." It is a way of you saying to the client that someone else, the story character with a similar and somewhat equivalent problem, has successfully resolved his dilemma. It is a motivational device that sets up the expectation in the client that he too can be just as successful with his own dilemma.

Although the construction materials that go into building a therapeutic metaphor are presented in a step-by-step manner, you may find that you prefer to organize your approach to the process differently. The carefully thought out logical sequence of construction steps that work for many may not work the same way for you. We do not always approach a concept from its beginning. At times, a metaphor may appear to you as a gestalt, whereby you see the whole structure at once and go back to add components that give it life. It is also possible to be struck with a resolution to the client's problem and work backward adding features where appropriate. Consequently, the value of this model of metaphor construction depends less on its order of building blocks, but rather on their utility.

Enhancements

After you have constructed the basic metaphor, you can breathe further life into your creation. How skillfully you master the following concepts will determine the effectiveness of your work with metaphors.

Points of Correspondence   PC

The extent to which a story character resembles a significant person in the client's life is always difficult to assess. As a general rule, the less distance between outward features of the metaphor character and the client, along with great emotional correspondence, the more effective the metaphor. For example, a butterfly emerging from its cocoon might be compared with an introverted young person discovering the joys of socializing, or the feeling of isolation and loneliness the caterpillar must be feeling in its cocoon are points of correspondence for the feelings of the client. However, if a client finds too obvious a comparison between himself and the story you are telling, the client may resign himself to the very resistance that prompted the metaphor in the first place. These points of correspondence require a delicate balance between the subtle and the obvious in terms of client recognition of comparison. To illustrate the importance of the element of points of correspondence is to metaphor, there is a story that went around at the height of the Beatles' popularity. Perhaps apocryphal, the story is about an opportunity they had to replace Ringo, who was considered the least popular Beatle. It seems, early in the band's career, Ringo had to leave the group for a weekend to fulfill a prior commitment to another band. The Beatles were able to attract the best drummer in England to replace him for the recording session that weekend. As it turned out, they chose to have Ringo continue as a Beatle. When comparing the two drummers, it turned out that apparently Ringo was more congruent with (although much less of a musician) and "corresponded" to what they believed the Beatles should be as a band.

The points of correspondence coincide with the similarities drawn from the behaviors of the client. Problems can arise when becoming too specific if you have little knowledge of what conforms to a client's life experience in a particular area. Therefore, it is best to give a general enough description in the metaphor so that the client is afforded the opportunity to mentally fill in details of the situation that are congruent with his own perceptions and beliefs.

Positive Expectations   PE

You can also set up a positive expectation for the client by including positive events that the story character experiences, which will be transferred through the client's ability to identify with that character. The client is further motivated to take positive action because the character has already benefited by taking a similar action in the story (the client being inspired to change by example). Another way to enhance a metaphor's effectiveness is to include direct statements of encouragement, support, and even direction to the client. This technique is called embedded suggestions and has been adapted from the hypnotherapy arena, where it serves to affect the behavior one who is in a trance state by entering the unconscious.

Embedded Suggestions   ES

The principle of the embedded suggestion, also known as "unconscious priming," is an effective way to convey a message within the body of a metaphor that doesn't appear on its surface to relate to the client, but relates to the client at an unconscious level. The unconscious is better able to sort out the content material that will better serve the client to deal with the presenting problem.

As Lankton (1980, p. 218) points out, "Therapists are advised not just to accept the client's conscious explanations: just content, the form of the process, and the structure of the experience is honestly offered up by everyone's unconscious." The mind picks up these embedded words or suggestions and translates them into a pattern that brings light to the client's presenting problem. Although this technique of embedding a suggestion in a metaphor differs from presenting the suggestion as a direct interpretation, keep in mind that the metaphor should always contain enough differences from the client's actual circumstances to avoid fostering resistance. Suggestions to a client that are embedded in the context of the metaphor can greatly motivate and support. Although it is helpful in some instances, a hypnotic trance is not needed to influence the unconscious.

The following metaphor is offered to better explain how a story character's situation may correspond to that of a client's, and to illustrate the inclusion of positive expectation and embedded suggestions. The metaphor was created for a troubled adolescent who was having extreme difficulty getting along with his father. The boy perceived his father as dictatorial and inflexible and refused to talk to him. He said that every time he and his father spoke he lost his autonomy and felt controlled by him. In order to try to reinstate the communication between father and son, I spoke to the boy about his favorite sport, baseball.

> There was a rookie outfielder who played for one of our minor league teams. He had a lot of potential and was coming up fast until one day he got hit with a pitched ball. I mean it hit him pretty hard, and he became

intimidated by this real fastball pitcher. The rookie would get into the batter's box but back off on every pitch. It was like not batting at all. But you see, this kid wanted to be a winner and took close instructions from his batting coach, who had faith that the young ballplayer would overcome his fears and start really playing ball. The coach said, "Keep calm when you get in there. You need to wait the pitcher out until he comes to you. You may need to give up a little control to the pitcher by keeping your eyes concentrating on the ball. You lean in if he throws an outside curve, and get the hell out of the way if he crowds you with an inside fastball. But eventually, if you hang in there, he'll have to come to you." And that's what happened. The young ballplayer did better and better, and made his opponent pitch to him, period. He got a lot of base hits and many home runs and earned their respect. He learned that he didn't need to be afraid of giving up a little control if he really was in control of himself. The young man turned out to be quite a winner. The young ballplayer: Pete Rose.

—Based on sports stories about Pete Rose

The opposing pitcher's actions correspond to the adolescent's father's abusive behavior, "hitting him pretty hard," and set the stage for the following enhancements. The embedded suggestions are, "Keep calm," "give up a little control," "hang in there," "took close instructions" from his batting coach (clinician), and "wait the pitcher out." The positive expectations, "did better and better," "got a lot of base hits and many home runs," and "earned the respect" of his opponents. You can clearly see how those components enhance the effectiveness of the therapeutic metaphor.

Both embedded suggestions and positive expectations support, encourage, and motivate. The former is a more direct statement to the client to take action, and the latter describes positive events that will occur when the client makes changes as modeled by the story character. A short example further illustrates these components.

A middle-aged man has been impotent since the dissolution of his bad marriage. He is now involved in what he describes as a satisfying relationship with "a lovely woman," yet the client remains impotent. One is his favorite activities is ballroom dancing. The following metaphor was told to the client.

> I have a friend who loves to dance . . . except he was going with this woman who was really clumsy on the dance floor. She had no grace and stepped on his feet continuously. She made it very difficult to enjoy dancing with her; they were really very out of tune. As they continued against his better judgment, he noticed that his dancing became less and less natural and spontaneous. It no longer was a lovely, smooth and easy experience, but became uncomfortable and even a little frustrating. He was becoming turned off to something that was normally a pleasurable experience for him. It got so bad that he actually stopped dancing, losing the desire completely. And he broke up with her. Well, he still avoided dancing for what seemed like a very long time, especially for one who is such a natural dancer. He turned down invitations from other women who also like to dance; he just wasn't up to it
>
> One day, however, he met a "super lady" who said that she loved dancing as much as he did. He began to feel the older rhythms coming back into his body. He then gave into his natural feelings and took her dancing. To his amazement, they seemed to fit perfectly into each other's bodies. She was a very good dancer, smooth and graceful . . . and fun. But as much is he wanted to, he found that he couldn't keep up with her. He was afraid, but didn't know exactly of what. "Perhaps I'll never be able to be the good dancer I once was" was a frightening thought that prevented him from continuing to dance. He felt he lost his sense of rhythm and timing after that lengthy bad experience. But with his girlfriend's help, he began to feel a lot better about dancing. He had a lot more ups and downs and slowly began to gain his self-confidence back. He began to relax and take it all in his stride. He found that he was a very natural dancer and gained back the ins and outs of ballroom dancing with

spontaneity and grace. He now danced with the ease and pleasure he had experienced before.

—Based on a metaphor by Joan Hersh, PhD

The points of correspondence in the above metaphor are aimed at the client's interest area of dancing, and are very specific: first girlfriend, but not wife, who was a bad partner; degeneration of the dancing activity after the marriage broke up; loss of desire for dancing and for a new intimate and sexual relationship. There is an embedded suggestion to "relax and take it all in his stride" and "began to gain his self-confidence back." The positive expectations that with his girlfriend's help he will gradually recover leaves enough room for the client to make his own associations to his sexual problems, which are never mentioned anywhere in the metaphor.

Following are two models that show how to put the therapeutic metaphor together from beginning to end. I designed this first therapeutic metaphor model to mainly illustrate components of points of correspondence that deal with characters, setting, place, time, interest areas, and vocabulary that the client can identify with. References are made in the annotation to other points of correspondence, such as embedded suggestions and positive expectations, and a full treatment of those components is reserved for the second therapeutic metaphor model.

Metaphor Model 1: James's Metaphor

James was referred to me by his internist for emotional problems stemming from his recent bankruptcy. James is 45 years old and the father of three. He is a college graduate and owns a service provider business.

James had done very well in his business for more than three years. He was encouraged to expand when a colleague offered him more business than his current organization could handle. He took out a substantial loan based upon the expected increase in business, moved into larger quarters, and hired additional help. For reasons not made clear to James, his colleague was unable to provide the amount of new business promised, so James needed to generate more business on his own to meet his higher expenses. He had a very difficult year, and was soon forced to declare bankruptcy.

James is suffering from many emotional problems; they include depression manifesting in difficulty sleeping, lack of concentration, and headaches. His diagnosis is major depressive episode. Some of his more pronounced symptoms are dysphoric mood characterized by feelings of hopelessness and guilt; he is currently on antidepressants.

His entire life has been detrimentally affected by his financial situation. He is in the process of losing his house, and there is little money for anything but survival needs. James's business is still functioning, but major work is required to reestablish even a minimum level of productivity.

James has had major relationship difficulties with his wife, which led her to threaten divorce. He is feeling desperate about her leaving. She has attended several co-joint sessions to talk about her feelings. James is maintaining a fairly good relationship with his children throughout. Yet one of his wife's complaints is that he isn't spending enough time with the children, and that she is taking the major responsibility for their discipline and guidance.

The client is very willing to participate in the therapy sessions. He is highly motivated to work at improving his situation, but he becomes overwhelmed with the perceived magnitude of his problems. He reports, "Every time things get a little better, something else comes crashing down on my head!" Below is James's metaphor.

> I read an article in the sport pages about Terry Bradshaw. Actually it was a story Terry told about his early experience with the Pittsburgh Steelers. I'm not sure if he said it was his second or third year, but it was a rough one, as he tells it. His team wasn't very together and he was getting clobbered in every game. Luckily the teams he played against that season had problems and his team got to the playoffs.
>
> The team he played against in the championship game was Miami and they were really tough. The Miami

Stadium was full to capacity and he felt the terrible pressure and stress to pull this one out. The crowd seemed to be screaming for his blood and screamed wildly whenever he was sacked. He kept getting knocked down every time he got the ball and couldn't understand why he was taking so much punishment. His team also felt demoralized and looked to him to turn it around and lead them to victory. There was nothing they could do without his leadership. He realized also that it was up to him to find a way out of the dilemma. He couldn't understand what was happening to turn things so against him and blames himself for not being good enough at his job. It got harder and harder to get up from the ground after each sack.

Then it happened. On that last play before the half, he went back to pass and didn't even see what hit him. He was knocked senseless and removed from the game. As he came around, he saw there were many people hovering around him, offering their support. One at a time, his teammates lined up to yell words of encouragement like, "I'm glad to see you're feeling better," and "You'll make it!" His coach went over what he thought was some of the wrong choices he was making and they agreed upon some new alternatives. He told Terry that he and his team had confidence that Terry would do the very best he knew how, and that would make all the difference. He believed that Terry was the high caliber player that could turn a losing situation into a victory just by taking action. He told Terry that he came to Miami to win the championship and sent him back onto the field saying, "You're a winner, let's do it!"

As Terry told it, it was because of his determination to get back in the game that his team responded with their best also. He showed real leadership and together with a new game plan in the second half, he slowly turned it around. The Steelers won in overtime when Terry threw a touchdown pass that sailed over 50 yards. It was the longest successful pass he ever threw in his professional career. He said that it was his determination to overcome what seemed like such a hopeless situation and the belief that he and his teammates had the ability to be a winner that made all the difference.

James's Therapeutic Metaphor: Annotated

PC: Points of Correspondence	SC: Scene Change	CH: Character
ES: Embedded Suggestion	SO: Successful Outcome	ST: Setting
PE: Positive Expectation	Voc: Familiar word or phrase	TM: Time

	Therapeutic Metaphor	Annotation
1	I read an article in the sports pages about Terry Bradshaw. Actually, it was a story Terry told about his early experience with the Pittsburg Steelers.	CH: James was a quarterback at Penn State; Terry Bradshaw quarterbacked the Pittsburgh Steelers
2	I'm not sure if he said it was his second or third year, but it was a rough one, as he tells it.	TM: Time frame set to correspond to James's business difficulties
3	His team wasn't very together and he was getting clobbered in every game.	PC: Describes similar troubled times. Voc: "wasn't very together," "clobbered," descriptive patter.
4	Luckily the teams he played against that season had problems and his team got to the playoffs.	ST: The "playoffs" (Voc: sport's term) is where James is in his life.
5	The team he played against in the championship game was Miami and they were really tough.	Voc: The word "tough" emphasizes the times he's going through.
6	The Miami Stadium was full to capacity and he felt the terrible pressure and stress to pull this one out.	ST: James experienced enormous "pressure and stress" from the IRS and his bankruptcy. Voc: "pull this one out," "screaming for his blood," and "sacked" are sport terms.

Therapeutic Metaphor	Annotation
7 He kept getting knocked down every time he got the ball and couldn't understand why he was taking so much punishment.	PC: He can identify with feelings of not understanding why these terrible things are happening to him.
8 His team also felt demoralized and looked to him to turn it around and lead them to victory. There was nothing they could do without his leadership. He realized also that it was up to him to find a way out of the dilemma.	ST: The situation was demoralizing for all. PC: Corresponds to James's acceptance that he has to take care of the "dilemma" that he and his family ("team") are in.
9 He couldn't understand what was happening to turn things so against him and blames himself for not being good enough at his job.	PC: James also experienced self-blame for his financial situation.
10 It got harder and harder to get up from the ground after each sack. Then it happened. On that last play before the half, he went back to pass and didn't even see what hit him. He was knocked senseless and removed from the game.	ST: Describes unexpected problem with his bankruptcy and the IRS. PC: James was unable to deal with the added pressure ("removed from the game") and was hospitalized.
11 As he came around, he saw there were many people hovering around him, offering their support. One at a time, his teammates lined up to yell words of encouragement like, "I'm glad to see you're feeling better," and "You'll make it!"	PE: Implies James will feel better, and is cared about by his family and friends who visited him in the hospital and encouraged him to get well soon.
12 His coach went over what he thought was some of the wrong choices he was making and they agreed upon some new alternatives. He told Terry that he and his team had confidence that Terry would do the very best he knew how, and that would make all the difference.	PE: Implies that the clinician (coach) and James will find new ways to cope with the situation. ES: Suggestion to do his "very best" for a different and positive outcome.

Therapeutic Metaphor	Annotation
13 He believed that Terry was the high caliber player that could turn a losing situation into a victory just by taking action.	PC: James identifying with Terry makes him also of "high caliber" and able to "take action" to "turn a losing situation into a victory."
14 He told Terry that he came to Miami to win the championship and sent him back onto the field saying, "You're a winner, let's do it!"	PE: Sets up expectations that James will deal successfully with his problem. ES: James is a "winner."
15 As Terry told it, it was because of his determination to get back in the game that his team responded with their best also. He showed real leadership and together with a new game plan in the second half, he slowly turned it around. The Steelers won in overtime when Terry threw a touchdown pass that sailed over 50 yards. It was the longest successful pass he ever threw in his professional career. He said that it was his determination to overcome what seemed like such a hopeless situation and the belief that he and his teammates had the ability to be a winner that made all the difference.	SO: Description of how James's efforts will bring success.

Metaphor Model 2: Lisa's Metaphor

Lisa is a woman in her forties I treated about a year before she returned. She does not have a job but is a stay-at-home mother. She leaves the house only for her shopping and therapy sessions. She is an extremely intelligent woman who graduated from an Ivy League university but dropped out of a graduate program in business administration when she lost her only child, a teenage son. He was a new driver who received his license only a week before his fatal automobile accident. It was raining and after dark when he begged his mother to let him use the car to see his girlfriend. "I knew I was doing the wrong thing," Lisa related, "but I just couldn't say 'no' to him. I could never say 'no' to him."

Lisa talked about the guilt she felt about not being the kind of parent who could control her son. She related that it was easier for her to deal with all the responsibilities of school, her marriage, her housekeeping, by "giving in" to her son's demands. "He wasn't a bad kid, but I didn't give him the time and guidance he needed."

Lisa's physician referred her to me to complete her mourning process and begin to live a productive life again. It was over two years ago that Lisa lost her son and she had seemed to be doing well coping with his premature death. Then, on what would have been his 21st birthday, she went into a severe decline and shut herself off from the world.

She also described herself as having no control over her own life and as feeling there was nothing to live for. She briefly mentioned thinking about taking her own life, but knew that wasn't the right answer for her with her religious beliefs. "I just don't know what to do with myself, God help me," she declared. Her relationship with her husband had deteriorated and she broke off contact with her family and friends. Below is Lisa's metaphor.

> Walking along the beach I chanced upon a turtle egg shimmering in the white sand. I stopped and watched as the egg seemed to take on motion and a tiny crack began to form on the side of the egg. I wondered what that little turtle must be thinking closed away in its dark prison. That poor little creature, unknowing about what awaits it once in the world of predators waiting for it to emerge from its shell. It must feel trapped and helpless. Things must look very black to that creature at that moment. And I wonder whether or not the turtle really knows about such a bright and interesting future in store for it in the beautiful ocean.
>
> Change is beginning to happen for the turtle in its shell. The shell is cracking and more light is shining through the opening. The turtle is wanting to escape from it shell. It keeps pushing to free itself from its dark existence. But nothing is really unusual about the turtle

emerging from its shell. It happens all the time. It's as natural as day following night. The turtle needs to emerge after a time of darkness to come into the light and face a wonderful life ahead of it. The turtle can't help becoming what it will be, God's creation coming into the world.

I have a friend Laura, who had planned her future in an exciting and successful way. She and her husband bought an old school bus and started converting it into a motor home. Their plan for future was to retire and travel around the U.S. visiting the many beautiful sites our country has to offer. Her husband did most of the work on it; and over time it began to take shape as a motor home. They changed it and fixed whatever needed correcting, in what seemed like 18 years. Most nights, every moment of spare time was poured diligently into the project. It was almost finished but there was still a lot of work to be done before it could be taken out on the road. Laura was realizing that the success of the project was also in her hands and began to take more responsibility for her part. Her husband worked on the engine to make sure it would be strong against all road hazards.

Then one day a tragedy. The garage caught fire. The fire tore through the garage and the motor home was beyond repair. Laura was obsessed with the thought that had they worked harder on the project, the motor home would have been completed much sooner and then safely stored on a parking lot. Her first reaction was that she was disturbed by losing the motor home prematurely. Then she was angry and frustrated that the family no longer will have the opportunity to travel together. And then she decided that she no longer wanted to think about the situation. Laura put it out of mind for what seemed like two years, but couldn't seem to get started on her own life. She kept coming back to the motor home and the failed plans for family travel together. She, again, began to enter into that dark space.

In a short time, the turtle freed itself from its prison and began its journey to the ocean. One can imagine how freeing it felt to emerge from the darkness into the light, and how hopeful the turtle must have been to swim in the sea. The turtle scurried as fast as he could to cross the hot sand to the cool waters. Laura began to dream again of the wonderful journeys she would be taking soon with her husband. She decided to continue her education and start a small business with her husband.

Yes, this was the perfect time for Laura to escape from her shell and enter into the light. Her past was pretty dark and her struggles difficult, but she decided she needed to make a positive move and change her life, and I'm happy to report that Laura and her husband did open a business which is still thriving today.

The accompanying annotation for the second metaphor is my attempt to illustrate the various components that were integrated into the content of the metaphor. I have made a great effort to include a complete enough description of the "enhancing" components to help you better understand the construction process. There are also enough "un-noted" components to allow you to make your own connections.

Lisa's Therapeutic Metaphor: Annotated

PC: Points of Correspondence	SC: Scene Change	CH: Character.
ES: Embedded Suggestion	SO: Successful Outcome	ST: Setting
PE: Positive Expectation	Voc: Familiar word or phrase	TM: Time

	Therapeutic Metaphor	Annotation
1	Walking along the beach I chanced upon a turtle egg shimmering in the white sand. I stopped and watched as the egg seemed to take on motion and a tiny crack began to form on the side of the egg. I wondered what that little turtle must be thinking closed away in its dark prison.	ST: The darkness and loneliness that must exist inside an egg is compared to Lisa's lonely, and fearful existence. Voc: Lisa used the phrase, "I feel like I'm in prison."

Therapeutic Metaphor	Annotation
2	That poor little creature, unknowing about what awaits it once in the world of predators waiting for it to emerge from its shell. It must feel trapped and helpless.	PC: Lisa complains that she doesn't have control over her life. Voc: "trapped and helpless"
3	Things must look very black to that creature at that moment.	PC: Corresponds to Lisa's present feelings.
4	And I wonder whether or not the turtle really knows about such a bright and interesting future in store for it in the beautiful ocean.	PE: Lisa's future can be "bright and interesting."
5	Change is beginning to happen for the turtle in its shell.	ES: Suggesting to Lisa that she is beginning to experience a change from her dark situation.
6	The shell is cracking and more light is shining through the opening. The turtle wants to escape from its shell. It keeps pushing to free itself.	PC: Lisa identifies with her present, wanting to escape from her misery. ES: Suggestion to start "pushing to free" herself from her dark existence.
7	But nothing is really unusual about the turtle emerging from its shell. It happens all the time. It's as natural as day following night. The turtle needs to emerge after a time of darkness to come into the light and face a wonderful life ahead of it.	ES: Change is a natural process and is always happening. PC: "The turtle needs to emerge" as Lisa needs to emerge "after a time of darkness." PE: And "face a wonderful life ahead."
8	The turtle can't help becoming what it will be, God's creation coming into the world.	PC: Corresponds to Lisa's religious beliefs that change will occur to bring her into the light with God's help.
9	I have a friend Laura, who had planned her future in an exciting and successful way.	SC: Story shifts to Lisa's plans to attend graduate school and on to the exciting world of business before her son's death. CH: Lisa can identify with Laura as corresponding character acting as a model who had similar plans for the future.

Therapeutic Metaphor	Annotation
10 She and her husband bought an old school bus and started converting it into a motor home. Their plan for the future was to retire and travel around the U.S. visiting the many beautiful sites our country has to offer.	PC: The motor home is a symbol for Lisa's plan to travel together with her son, a wish often repeated in therapy. CH: Lisa's husband ST: Corresponds to the couple's often talked about plans to have the family travel together.
11 Her husband did most of the work on it; and over time it began to take shape as a motor home.	PC: Lisa recognizes that she did not fully participated in her son's upbringing.
12 They changed it and fixed whatever needed correcting, in what seemed like 18 years. Most nights, every moment of spare time was poured diligently into the project. It was almost finished but there was still a lot of work to be done before it could be taken out on the road.	TM: Their son was 18 when he died. ES: Lisa had a lot of work to do to deal with her problems, but working "diligently" would be needed.
13 Laura was realizing that the success of the project was also in her hands and began to take more responsibility for her part.	ES: Suggestion that Lisa take more responsibility for responsibility for her life.
14 Her husband worked on the engine to make sure it would be strong against all road hazards.	PC: Lisa knows how her husband gave great attention to their son and she did not.
15 Then one day a tragedy. The garage caught fire.	SC: A sudden change in life plans similar to her own. Voc: "a tragedy"
16 The fire tore through the garage and the motor home was beyond repair.	PC: The son was killed in a car accident. Voc: "vehicle beyond repair"
17 Laura was obsessed with the thought that had they worked harder on the project, the motor home would have been completed much sooner and then safely stored on a parking lot.	PC: Lisa blames herself for not giving her son more time and guidance. She stated that if she had been able to just say "no" to her son, the tragedy would have been prevented.

Therapeutic Metaphor	Annotation
18 Her first reaction was that she was disturbed by losing the motor home prematurely. Then she was angry and frustrated that the family no longer will have the opportunity to travel together. And then she decided that she no longer wanted to think about the situation.	PC: Describes the many conflicting thoughts and feelings Lisa is dealing with.
19 Laura put it out of mind for what seemed like two years, but couldn't seem to get started on her own life. She kept coming back to the motor home and the failed plans for family travel together. She, again, began to enter into that dark space.	PC: Lisa entered into a state of denial for a long time until she became depressed and was referred to therapy. ST: "that dark space"
20 In a short time, the turtle freed itself from its prison and began its journey to the ocean.	SC: Brings Lisa back to the turtle image. PE: Lisa freeing herself from her dark past. ES: It is time for her to begin her "journey" back to health.
21 One can imagine how freeing it felt to emerge from the darkness into the light, and how hopeful the turtle must have been to swim in the sea.	ES: Lisa's depression can be lifted and she will emerge from the "darkness into the light." PE: Engenders hope that Lisa will have her life back again.
22 The turtle scurried as fast as he could to cross the hot sand to the cool waters.	ES: Suggestion to not hesitate to begin the healing process.
23 Laura began to dream again of the wonderful journeys she would be taking soon with her husband. She decided to continue her education and start a small business with her husband.	SC: Brings Lisa back to the work she needs to do with her husband in the future. ES: Lisa is prompted to "make a decision" whether to return to her graduate program or find some other means of improving her life.

Therapeutic Metaphor	Annotation
24 Yes, this was the perfect time for Laura to escape from her shell and enter into the light. Her past was pretty dark and her struggles difficult, but she decided she needed to make a positive move and change her life, and I'm happy to report that Laura and her husband did open a business which is still thriving today.	ES: To again reinforce the suggestion to make a positive "move" to change her situation. PC: Confirm and validate that Lisa had difficult struggles in her past. Voc: "positive move," "change" SO: Description of Laura and her husband's efforts brought success.

At this point, I believe I have provided a workable model of therapeutic metaphor so you can understand and construct metaphors that will fit the needs of your clients. Further explanation, commentary or analysis, can only detract from its existing wholeness. The following Sufi tale is most appropriate here.

A little boy captured a fly.

Being a curious child

he took the fly apart,

trying to understand how it was put together.

Well, he pulled the fly into pieces,

and had the wings, and the legs,

and the body and the head . . .

And wondered where the fly had gone.

Appendix A

Extended Metaphor Examples from Literature

IN "EXTENDED METAPHOR EXAMPLES from Literature," Hassler (2014) explicates "The Road Not Taken" by Robert Frost: "In his famous poem, 'The Road Not Taken,' Robert Frost uses an extended metaphor to compare two roads to various life paths and the weighty decision of which direction to follow."

> Two roads diverged in a yellow wood,
> And sorry I could not travel both
> And be one traveler, long I stood
> And looked down one as far as I could
> To where it bent in the undergrowth;
> Then took the other, as just as fair,
> And having perhaps the better claim,
> Because it was grassy and wanted wear;
> Though as for that the passing there
> Had worn them really about the same,
> And both that morning equally lay
> In leaves no step had trodden black.
> Oh, I kept the first for another day!
> Yet knowing how way leads on to way,
> I doubted if I should ever come back.
> I shall be telling this with a sigh
> Somewhere ages and ages hence:
> Two roads diverged in a wood, and I—
> I took the one less travelled by,
> And that has made all the difference.

Hassler continues, "Frost is comparing life journeys and experiences to roads that are traveled or bypassed. Frost is reflecting on this monumental decision later in life and 'ages and ages' since he made his choice. This shows that wisdom has confirmed that choosing one's path will affect the rest of one's life—as taking the less worn road has affected him tremendously."

You can choose from a wealth of examples of extended metaphors in literature to use or modify to address your client's problem. Use your experiences to image how you could use the following metaphors in your practice:

In Greek mythology, Icarus, accused of hubris, ignored warnings and flew too close to the sun; when the wax in his wings melted he tumbled out of the sky and fell into the sea.

Metaphors from novels like *The Great Gatsby* by F. Scott Fitzgerald tell of the (human) poverty in the "Valley of Ashes."

An Aesop's fable like "The Boy Who Cried Wolf" works well to have the client recognize the consequences of his or her behavior as it affects those around him at home and in his community.

The clinician recounting for the client parts of a film or a play that corresponds to the client's experience serves this purpose. The film "To Kill a Mockingbird," from the novel by Harper Lee, serves as a metaphor for a client who, like lawyer Atticus Finch who goes up against a racist society in defense of a black man, faces prejudices from his community.

Plays like "The Phantom of the Opera" (Broadway's longest-running hit), based on the novel by Gaston Leroux, present the story of the heroine, Christine, who "sticks with" a man who can't control his jealousy.

In the arts, Pablo Picasso's painting *Guernica* serves as a metaphor in the world of Art. Painted in June 1937 by Picasso in his home in Paris in response to the bombing by Nazi Germany and Fascist Italy of the Basque village from which the work took its name. *Guernica* also challenges its viewers in the best way, looking almost playful at first glance but almost immediately demanding that they confront the horror it actually contains. "A realistic image of the bombing of the town of *Guernica*, with corpses and screams in the night, would likely have felt melodramatic, saccharine, difficult to look at," writes Noah Charney. He goes on to say, "It might have been Romanticized or it might have been so gritty that our reaction would be to shut down our ability to sympathize, as a defense mechanism. The figures are almost cartoonish, but then of course, when you look more closely, when you know the context, they are not. But the childlike abstraction pulls us in, whereas the same subject, handled as a photorealist blood-fest, would repel us."

Appendix B

Metaphor Forms

THESE DEFINITIONS ARE ADAPTED from *Short Story and the Oral Tradition,* by Paul C. Sherr (1970).

Allegory

A literary device that constructs parallels between objects or persons or both. Because it substitutes one thing for another, an allegory is in essence an extended metaphor. To use a pig as a stand-in for a man is to suggest that a man behaves like a pig. To equate the month of May with a man's entrance into the joys of maturity and equate the month of September with his entry into old age is to establish the cycle of the year as parallel to the cycle of life.

Anecdote

A short, prescriptive narrative, relating a single incident in the affairs of a famous person. The outstanding characteristic of the anecdote is that clear-cut victory for the hero, usually at the expense of regulated and established authority.

Epic

Within the confines of article writing, for example, the epic incorporates through a series of episodes of the characteristics of a nation or race as prescribed by a central figure of heroic proportion. Epics present the dynamic accomplishments of man for his own edification.

Metaphor Forms

Fable

Brief, pointed narrative that calls into question men's behavior on those occasions when he deludes himself. Including many types of characters: men, beasts, inanimate objects, gods, and nature. Fables are fundamentally satiric and didactic.

Fairy tale

A form of folktale in which supernatural figures—elves, gnomes, fairies, giants—intrude in the affairs of men for good or evil.

Folktale

Any of the seven types of stories that deal fundamentally with the hopes and aspirations of the common people, or folk. These stories are opposed to authority figures, usually royalty, but also any type of superior being: giants, police, military figures, or such animals as the lion.

Joke. A brief narrative, ending with a humorous, unexpected twist, characterized by ribaldry and coarseness. Placed in a larger context, jokes serve to avoid or put off conflict.

Myth

A collection of tales that attempt to answer man's questions about natural phenomena, such as the sequence of night and day, the change of the seasons, or the cycle of birth, life, death.

Parable

An allegorical story with a deliberately enigmatic message, thereby allowing for free interpretation.

Satire

A literary device, and by extension a literary work, that uses laughter to call man's attention to his self-delusions in the hope that he will make a change for the better.

Appendix C

My Bell Jar *of Useful Metaphors*

YOU CAN USE METAPHORS from books and the Internet with your clients. Several collected here can be successful when treating problems from anxiety and depression, to interpersonal relationships, to post-traumatic stress disorder.

A reminder: You may choose to tell them as they are, or modify them to suit the individual needs of your clients.

A metaphor for strengthening a dysfunctional family through unity and openness to the other.

The Father and His Sons

A father had a family of sons who were perpetually quarreling among themselves. When he failed to heal their disputes by his exhortations, he determined to give them a practical illustration of the evils of disunion. For this purpose, one day he told them to bring him a bundle of sticks tied tightly together. When they had done so, he placed the bundle into the hands of each of them in succession, and ordered them to break it in pieces. They tried with all their strength, and were not able to do it. He next opened the bundle, took the sticks separately, one by one, and again put them into his sons' hands, upon which they broke them easily. He then addressed them in these words: "My sons, if you are of one mind, and unite to assist each other, you will be as this strong bundle, uninjured by all the attempts of your enemies; but if you are divided among yourselves, you will be broken as easily as these sticks."

—An Aesop Fable

*Life will, at times, bring difficulties down on you.
Your client will see that even adversity can be a
stepping-stone to success. It is a reminder that it's not
what happens to you, but how you react to it.*

The Farmer's Donkey—A Fable

One day a farmer's donkey fell down into a well. The animal cried piteously for hours as the farmer tried to figure out a way to get him out. Finally he decided it was probably impossible and the animal was old and the well was dry anyway, so it just wasn't worth it to try to retrieve the donkey. So the farmer asked his neighbors to come over and help him cover up the well. They all grabbed shovels and began to shovel dirt into the well.

At first, when the donkey realized what was happening he cried horribly. Then, to everyone's amazement, he quieted down and let out some happy brays. A few shovel loads later, the farmer looked down the well to see what was happening and was astonished at what he saw. With every shovel of dirt that hit his back, the donkey was shaking it off and taking a step up. As the farmer's neighbors continued to shovel dirt on top of the animal, he continued to shake it off and take a step up. Pretty soon, to everyone's amazement, the donkey stepped up over the edge of the well and trotted off!

Moral: Life is going to shovel dirt on you. The trick to getting out of the well is to shake it off and take a step up. Every adversity can be turned into a stepping-stone. The way to get out of the deepest well is by never giving up but by shaking yourself off and taking a step up.

You can include the moral if you like. I usually don't include it in the original telling, but wait for a response, if any, from the client. Then I go back to the metaphor, announce it as the "moral," and ask for another response.

—Source unknown

The Starfish metaphor can help your clients understand that we have the power to change another's life through our perseverance, and against great difficulty and criticism; it gives them insight and motivation.

The Starfish Parable

One day, an old man was walking along a beach that was littered with thousands of starfish that had been washed ashore by the high tide. As he walked he came upon a young boy who was eagerly throwing the starfish back into the ocean, one by one.

Puzzled, the man looked at the boy and asked what he was doing. Without looking up from his task, the boy simply replied, "I'm saving these starfish, Sir."

The old man chuckled aloud, "Son, there are thousands of starfish and only one of you. What difference can you make?"

The boy picked up a starfish, gently tossed it into the water and, turning to the man, said, "I made a difference to that one!"

—Source unknown

The folktale "Stone Soup" provides your client with a description of the power of human resilience and ingenuity. It motivates the client to change one's personal difficult circumstances through self-reliance, and by enlisting the best instincts of people in the community.

The Stone Soup folktale

There once was a traveler who came to a small village, tired and weary from his long journey. The traveler did not have anything to eat and hoped that a friendly villager would be able to feed him. He came to the first house and knocked on the door. He asked the woman who answered if she could spare just a small bit of food as he had traveled a long journey and was very hungry. The woman replied, "I'm sorry I have nothing to give you. I can barely feed my own family."

So the traveler went to another door and asked again. The answer was the same: "I have nothing to give you." He went from door to door and each time was turned away.

Undaunted, the traveler went to the village square, took a small tin cooking pot from his bag, filled it with water, started a fire and dropped a stone in the pot. As he boiled the water, a passing villager stopped and asked him what he was doing. The traveler replied, "I'm making stone soup. Would you like to join me?" The villager said yes, and he asked if carrots were good in stone soup. "Sure," said the traveler. The villager went home and returned with carrots from his garden to add to the boiling water.

Soon, another curious villager came by and was invited to join them. She went home and returned with some potatoes. A young boy passed by and soon joined the group, bringing his mother and dinner plates from their home.

In time, a crowd gathered with everyone offering their own favorite ingredient: mushrooms, onions, salt, black pepper, acorn squash. Everyone wanted to be part of the creation.

Finally, the traveler removed the stone and declared, "The stone soup is ready!" And the whole community joined in a feast where there was none before.

—Adapted from Marcia Brown's retelling of the fable in her book, *Stone Soup: An Old Tale*.)

A metaphor to help your client face adversity and see the problem through to a successful ending.

You might say, "There's a poem by Edgar Guest that I like to read aloud to myself when things aren't going so well for me. It's called 'See It Through.' May I share it with you?"

See It Through

When you're up against a trouble,
Meet it squarely, face to face;
Lift your chin and set your shoulders,
Plant your feet and take a brace.
When it's vain to try to dodge it,
Do the best that you can do;
You may fail, but you may conquer,
See it through!

Black may be the clouds about you
And your future may seem grim,
But don't let your nerve desert you;
Keep yourself in fighting trim.
If the worst is bound to happen,
Spite of all that you can do,
Running from it will not save you,
See it through!

Even hope may seem but futile,
When with troubles you're beset,
But remember you are facing
Just what other men have met.
You may fail, but fall still fighting;
Don't give up, whate'er you do;
Eyes front, head high to the finish.
See it through!

This is a wonderful metaphor to use with overbearing parents whose children desperately need to have their parents recognize their potential and believe in them.

MY BELL JAR OF USEFUL METAPHORS

Planting a Bean Seed

When my now 19-year-old daughter (use the gender and age of the client's child) was in Grade 3, all of Mrs. Matthews' students were given a small pot with a bean seed to plant. Green string beans it seems are pretty hardy and the perfect seed to use when promoting green thumbs in young children. That same plant was also a most unexpected source of understanding and insight for me. Once the bean plants had sprouted and flowered, that teacher allowed the kids to carefully transfer the precious cargo from school to home. Once home, Shanna scouted around for the perfect location and settled on a sunny south windowsill and then proudly declared, "Soon I can feed the whole family!"

Noticing our cat looking intrigued should have been a warning to me because when I woke up the next morning, I saw that the bean plant had been knocked off the windowsill and ripped from its pot. Its leaves were frayed and, except for a limp thread of stem that still connected the roots to the flowering top, it was quite unrecognizable from the day before. The plant, it seemed, was a goner. I dreaded what I had to tell Shanna but as I gently began to explain that the bean plant had to be put in the compost, her reaction was not what I expected. She said, "Everything will be okay, Mom, the plant will get better." Without wasting a second she secured the first aid kit from the bathroom and returned with gauze, a tongue depressor, bandages, and a deep belief that the pathetic looking, near-dead bean plant would live, thrive, and even produce food!

I had mixed emotions knowing that she was postponing the plant's inevitable trip to the compost bin, but I went along with it and helped her wrap bandages. Days later, to my absolute surprise, the bean plant was standing tall and looking perky. We were able to remove the bandages and discover a protruding hump in the stem where its near-fatal stem break had been. It was also amazing to see that the one and only bean, had become plump and a new sliver of green where a second bean was forming. I was excited and amazed while Shanna had been expecting nothing less.

I set the table beautifully with all the fanfare of a Thanksgiving dinner. The beans were carefully divided by 5, which awarded each person two small pieces, claw marks and all. They turned out to be the best green beans I had ever eaten!

My daughter never quite understood my exuberance over the significance of the beans. Now, more than ever, I see all my children, no exceptions, with the same eyes and heart that my daughter used on her broken, beaten up bean plant.

—Based on a story by Monique Howat

This joke/metaphor has been going around about not procrastinating and seizing opportunity when it arises.

The Fiddler on the Roof

An observant man was caught in a rainstorm and just about made it home before the waters began to rise. The rainstorm became stronger and after a few hours the man's house became flooded. The water rose and the man climbed to the roof and started praying. "Lord, please save me so I can continue praising your virtues."

At that moment, a Coast Guard rescue party floated by in a rowboat. "Come down now, get into the boat."

"No sir, I will stay here, replied the man, "I am sure that my Lord will stop the rain and save me."

An hour later, a second boat approached as the water approached the roof. "Sir, get in quickly."

"Thank you but I will stay here. The Lord will provide. I am certain that the rain will stop any minute."

A couple of hours later the roof was almost completely under water. The man was now clinging to the peak of the roof. A helicopter approached the roof. "Sir, grab on to the line. We will pull you up," a voice is heard on a loudspeaker.

"No please go, I'm all right. My Lord will provide," said the man as he looked heavenward. After the helicopter flew away, lightning hit the man and killed him. He arrived, furious, at the

Pearly Gates. "Why did this happen?" he shouted. "I thought, Lord, you would provide!" Then he heard a thunderous voice.

"Why in heaven's name were you fiddling around? I sent you two boats and a chopper."

—Source unknown

This metaphor is designed to address a disability that hinders a client's ability to move his life forward. In the story the young man's biggest weakness becomes his greatest strength.

Strength versus Weakness

Here is the story of a young man who decided to study a martial art in spite of the fact that he had lost his left arm in a devastating car accident. The boy began lessons with an old Japanese martial arts master. The boy was doing well, so he couldn't understand why, after three months of training, the master had taught him only one move.

"Sensei, honorable teacher," the boy finally said, "Shouldn't I be learning more moves?"

"This is the only move you know, but this is the only move you'll ever need to know," the sensei replied.

Not quite understanding, but believing in his teacher, the boy kept training.

Several months later, the sensei took the boy to his first tournament. Surprising himself, the boy easily won his first two matches. The third match proved to be more difficult, but after some time, his opponent became impatient and charged; the boy deftly used his one move to win the match. Still amazed by his success, the boy was now in the finals.

This time, his opponent was bigger, stronger, and more experienced. For a while, the boy appeared to be overmatched. Concerned that the boy might get hurt, the referee called a time-out. He was about to stop the match when the sensei intervened.

"No," the sensei insisted, "Let him continue."

Soon after the match resumed, his opponent made a critical mistake; He dropped his guard and instantly, the boy used his move to pin him. The boy had won the match and the tournament. He was the champion.

On the way home, the boy and the sensei reviewed every move in each and every match. Then the boy summoned the courage to ask what was really on his mind.

"Sensei, how did I win the tournament with only one move?"

"You won for two reasons," the sensei answered. "First, you've almost mastered one of the most difficult throws in all of judo. And second, the only known defense for that move is for your opponent to grab your left arm."

—Based on an Aikido tale

This metaphor exposes "self-importance" at the expense of others.

Change Your Course, Now!

The ship, USS Abraham Lincoln, was at sea in a heavy fog bad with visibility near zero. Suddenly the lookout on the bridge cried, "I can see a light far in the distance." The captain shouted to the signalman, "Signal the other ship: We are on a collision course. You need to change your course 15 degrees. "The signal that came back said, "You are advised to change your course 15 degrees!" The captain said to the signalman, "Send: This is the ship's captain. Change your course 15 degrees immediately to avoid collision!"

"No, I repeat, you change your course immediately to avoid collision!" came the reply.

The captain became furious. He said to the signalman, "Send: This is an aircraft carrier, the second largest ship in the United States' Atlantic fleet. We are accompanied by three destroyers, three cruisers and numerous support vessels. I demand that you change your course 15 degrees north. That's one-five degrees north, or counter measures will be undertaken to ensure the safety of this ship.

Then came the signal from the other.

"This is a lighthouse! Your call!"
—Source unknown

Being responsible to others has good returns.

The Secret of Growing Good Corn

Once there was a farmer who grew corn in his lands. Each year, his corn won first place in the state fair. One year, when the fair was over, a journalist asked him what the secret of his success was. The farmer revealed to the journalist that one of his success factors was that he shared seed corn with his neighbors. The journalist was surprised. "Why do you share your best seed corn with the neighbors? Each year they are entering corn in competition with yours!" the journalist said. "Didn't you know," said the farmer, "the wind picks up pollen from the ripening corn, then it swirls it around, from field to field. If the neighbors grow inferior corn, it is certain that cross-pollination will eventually degrade the quality of my corn. So it is smarter to help my neighbors grow good corn too, if I want to keep growing good, award-winning corn."
—Source unknown

A metaphor to express the selfless actions to help others through their suffering and pain.

The Only Window

Two seriously ill men occupied the same hospital room. The man who had his bed next to the only window would sit up and gaze out for hours. Unfortunately, the other man could not move and had to be flat on his back. They passed the time with one man describing to the other all the things he saw outside the window. "What lovely weather. You should see this beautiful park across the street and its lovely lake filled with ducks. There are kids sailing their boats and a couple walking arm-in-arm on a path full of flowers. In the distance you can see a great view of the city skyline."

Every day the man by the window would describe activities in the park, and the man on the other side of the room would close his eyes and imagine the scene, which helped him feel better and be more positive about life.

A few weeks later the man by the window died peacefully in his sleep. The other man asked to be moved next to the window. The nurse made the switch and slowly and painfully, the man propped himself up on one elbow. He was excited to take his first look at the park and the world outside. But he saw no park, no children, no lake, and no city skyline.

What he saw was a blank wall.

—Source unknown

A well-worn metaphor on being different and having self-worth.

A Colorful Balloon

An old man in the city center was selling colorful balloons. To attract the attention of children, once in a while he would release a helium filled balloon into the air. The children who saw that balloon go up, would get excited and ask their parents to buy one. While he was busy observing the crowd, a little dark-skinned boy approached him. The boy pulled his shirt. The man noticed the boy and smiled at him. "What can I do for you, little friend?" the man asked the boy. "I have a question to ask," replied the boy. "You released a yellow balloon and it flew high. Then a red balloon, a green balloon, a white balloon. They all flew high. If you release a black balloon, would that also fly high?" The balloon man was surprised to hear the boy's question. Then his eyes fell on the boy's dark skin, and he understood the question! The man smiled at the boy with affection and replied, "Son, it is not the color of the balloon; it is what's inside it that makes it go up!" and then he released a black balloon, which went up as high as the other balloons, and even further.

—Source unknown

Managing problems we encounter daily with
persistence, tenacity, and "doggedness."

The Persistent Bulldog

A man had two pedigreed setters that he trained to be bird dogs fenced in his backyard. One morning a little dog saw the two dogs and squeezed under the fence. The man thought he should remove the setters so they wouldn't hurt the little dog, but changed his mind. Maybe they would "teach that bulldog a lesson," he thought.

As he predicted, fur began to fly, and all of it was bulldog fur. The feisty intruder soon had enough and squeezed back under the fence to get away. To the man's surprise, the visitor returned again the next morning. He crawled under the fence and once again took on the tag-team of setters. And like the day before, he soon quit and squeezed out of the pen. The incident was repeated the following day, with the same results. The man left early the next morning on a business trip and returned after several weeks. He asked his wife what finally became of the bulldog. "You won't believe it," she replied. "Every day that little dog came to the backyard and fought with our setters. He never missed a day! It has come to the point now that when our setters simply hear him snorting down the alley, they start whining and run down into the basement. Then the little bulldog struts around our backyard as if he owns it."

In the end, it's the persistent bulldog that will own the backyard.

—Based on a story by Vicki Huffman

This metaphor can be used with a person (adult or
child) who is very argumentative, even aggressive,
and has difficulty controlling his/her temper.

The One You Feed

A young boy visited his Grandfather and told him that he was angry with a friend at school who played a mean trick on him. The Grandfather answered, "I will tell you a story about two wolves. I know exactly how these feelings are, it has happened to me, this hate of another. Imagine that two wolves live inside you. A good wolf that does no harm and will fight only if it is right to do so. The other wolf, the bad wolf, is full of anger and bad temper. He fights everyone for no reason, but his anger changes nothing. Instead, this wolf will end up having no friends. It is really hard for you to live with these two wolves inside, as they both try to control you."

The boy looked at his Grandfather's and asked, "Which wolf wins, Grandfather?"

The old man smiled. "The one you feed."

—Of Cherokee origin

References

Ahlhalau, (2014, June 20). "Two monks and a woman—a Zen Lesson." Retrieved from http://www.kindspring.org/story/view.php?sid=63753

Asch, S. E. (1958). The metaphor: The psychological inquiry. In R. Tagiuri & L. Petrullo (Eds.), *Person perception and interpersonal behavior*. Stanford, CA: Stanford University Press.

Bandler, R. & Grinder, J. (1975). *Patterns of the hypnotic techniques of Milton H. Erickson, M.D., Vol. I*. Cupertino, CA: Meta Publications.

Billow, R. M. (1977). Metaphor: A review of the psychological literature. *Psychological Bulletin*, 84(1), 81–92.

Billow, R. M. (1975). A cognitive developmental study of metaphor comprehension. *Developmental Psychology*, 11: 415–423.

Black, M. (1962). *Models and metaphors: Studies in languages and philosophy*. Ithaca, NY: Cornell University Press, .

Brooks, C. (1971). Irony as a principle of structure. In D. H. Richter (Ed.), *The critical tradition* (pp. 799–806). New York: Bedford/St. Martins.

Brown, M. (1947). *Stone soup: An old tale*. New York: Charles Scribner's Sons.

Buber, M. (1958). *Hasidism and modern man*. New York: Horizon Press.

Burke, K. (1945). *A grammar of motives*. New York: Prentice-Hall.

Charney, N. (April 30, 2017) Picasso's weapon against fascism: Why "Guernica" is the greatest of all war paintings. Retrieved from http://www.salon.com/2017/04/30/picassos-weapon-against-fascism-why-guernica-is-the-greatest-of-all-war-paintings/

Cohen, T. (1976). Notes on metaphor. *The Journal of Aesthetics and Art Criticism*, 34, 249–59.

Duhl, B. S. (1983). *From the inside out and other metaphors: Creative and integrative approaches to training in systems thinking*. New York: Bruner Meisel U.

Erickson, M. H. (1980). In E. L. Rossi (Ed.), *The collected papers of Milton H. Erickson on hypnosis*. New York: Irvington.

Friedberg, R. D. & Wilt, L. H. (2010). Metaphors and stories in cognitive behavioral therapy with children. *Journal of Rational-Emotive & Cognitive-Behavior Therapy*, 28(2), pp. 100–113.

Goodman, N. (1976). *Languages of Art*. Cambridge, MA: Hackett.

Gordon, D. (1978). *Therapeutic Metaphors*. Cupertino, CA: Meta Publications.

Guest, E. (n.d.). See it through. Retrieved from https://www.poetryfoundation.org/poems/44318/see-it-through

Haley, J. (1976). *Problem-solving therapy*. San Francisco: Jossey-Bass.

REFERENCES

Hassler, M. (2014, March 27). Extended metaphor examples from literature [Web log post]. Retrieved from https://webcache.googleusercontent. com/search?q=cache:ciXoOwKyq2kJ:https://blog.udemy.com/extended-metaphor-examples/+&cd=4&hl=en&ct=clnk&gl=us.

Howat, M. (n.d.). Positive inspirational persistence stories. Retrieved from http://www.agiftofinspiration.com.au/stories/persistence/Spark.shtml.

Huffman, V. (1989). *Plus living: Looking for joy in all the right places.* Wheaton, IL: Harold Shaw.

Johnson, M. (1981). *Philosophical perspectives on metaphor.* Minneapolis: University of Minnesota Press.

Kaplan, B. (1955). Some psychological methods for the investigation of expressive language. In H. Werner (Ed.), *On Expressive Language.* Worcester, MA: Clark University Press.

Kaufman, R. (1931) in J. M. Murry, *Countries of the mind: Essays in literary criticism* (pp. 1–2), 2nd series. London, England: Oxford University Press.

Kopp, S. (1971). *Guru: Metaphors from a psychotherapist.* Palo Alto, CA: Science and Behavior Books.

Kopp, S. (1972). *If you meet the Buddha on the road, kill him.* New York: Bantam Books.

Kövecses, Z. (2002). *Metaphor: A practical introduction* (2nd ed.). New York: Oxford University Press.

Lakoff, G. & Johnson, M. (1980). *Metaphors we live by.* Chicago: University of Chicago Press.

Lankton, S. R. & Lankton, C. H. (1983). *The answer within: A clinical framework of Ericksonian hypnotherapy.* NewYork: Brunner/Mazel.

Lankton, S. R. (1980). *Practical magic: A translation of basic neuro-linguistic programming into clinical psychotherapy.* Cupertino, CA: Meta Publications.

La Valle, Johns, (2016, November 08) "NLP is not therapy. Period!" [Web log post] Retrieved from https://www.purenlp.com.

Lenrow, P. B. (1966). Use of metaphor in facilitating constructive behavior change. *Psychotherapy: Theory, Research & Practice, 3*(4), 145–148.

Lewis, C. D. (1977). Metaphor was the beginning of wisdom. In Z. Radman (Ed.), *Metaphors: Figures of the mind.* London, England: Kluwer Academic Publishers.

Lewis, C. S. (1969). *Selected literary essays.* London, England: Cambridge University Press.

Miall, David S. (Ed.). (1982). *Metaphor, problems and perspectives.* Brighton, Sussex, England: Harvester Press, Atlantic Highlands, NJ: Humanities Press.

Moser, K. S. (1998). *Metaphor analysis in psychology—Method, theory, and fields of application* (Dissertation). Universität Zürich, Zürich, Lengerich: Pabst Science Publishers, Psychologia Universalis Series, p.21.

Murry, J. M. (1931). *Countries of the mind.* London, England: Oxford University Press.

References

Nietzsche, F. (1931). In J. M. Murry, *Countries of the mind* (pp. 1–2). London, England: Oxford University Press.

Nietzsche, F. (1995). *Philosophical writings*. New York: Bloomsbury Academic.

Ortony, A. (1975). Why metaphors are necessary and not just nice. *Educational Theory*. 25, 45–53.

Ortony, A. (Ed.) (1979). *Metaphor and thought*. New York:Cambridge University Press.

Paivio, A. & Walsh, M. (1979). Psychological Processes and Metaphor Comprehension. In A. Ortony (Ed.), *Metaphor and thought*, (pp. 307–328). New York: Cambridge University Press.

Perls, F. (1969). *Gestalt therapy verbatim*. Lafayette, CA: Real People Press.

Resnick, R. W. (1975). Chicken soup is poison. In F. D. Stephenson (Ed.), *Gestalt therapy primer*. Springfield, IL, Thomas.

Reynolds, R. E., & Schwartz, R. M. (1983). Relation of metaphoric processing to comprehension and memory. *Journal of Educational Psychology*, 75(3), 450–459.

Richards, I. A. (1929). *Practical criticism*. New York: Routledge.

Richards, I. A. (1936). *The philosophy of rhetoric*. London, England: Oxford University Press.

Ricoeur, P. (1977). *The rule of metaphor: Multi-disciplinary studies of the creation of meaning in language*. Toronto: University of Toronto Press.

Ritchie, L. D. (2013). *Metaphor*. New York: Cambridge University Press, .

Rogers, Robert (1978). *Metaphor: A psychoanalytic view*. Berkeley, CA: University of California Press.

Ross, W. D. & Smith, J. A. (Eds.). (1952). *The works of Aristotle*. Oxford, England: Clarendon Press.

Russo, J. P. (2015). *I. A. Richards: His life and work*. New York: Routledge Revivals.

Scott, Richard (2010). *Oxford guide to metaphors in CBT: Building cognitive bridges*. NewYork: Oxford University Press.

Shelley, P. B. (n.d.) A defense of poetry. Retrieved from http://www.bartleby.com/27/23.html

Sherr, P. C. (1970). *The short story and the oral tradition*. San Francisco: Boyd & Fraser.

Skinner, B. F. (1971). *Beyond freedom and dignity*. New York: Alfred A. Knopf.

Smith, N. L. (1981). *New perspectives in evaluation*. Thousand Oaks, CA: Sage.

Torneke, Niklas, (2017). *Metaphor in Practice*. Oakland, CA: New Harbinger Publications, Inc.

Tourangeau, R. & Sternberg, R. J. (1981). What makes a good metaphor. *Cognitive Psychology*, 13, 27–55.

Zeig, J. (1980). *A teaching seminar with Milton H. Erickson*. New York: Brunner/Mazel.

www.ingramcontent.com/pod-product-compliance
Lightning Source LLC
Chambersburg PA
CBHW072208270326
41930CB00011B/2575